Shouting Above the Noisy Crowd:

Biblical Wisdom and the Urgency of

Preaching

LLOYD JOHN OGILVIE INSTITUTE
OF PREACHING SERIES

SERIES EDITORS:

Mark Labberton
Clayton J. Schmit

The vision of the Lloyd John Ogilvie Institute of Preaching is to proclaim Jesus Christ and to catalyze a movement of empowered, wise preachers who seek justice, love mercy, and walk humbly with God, leading others to join in God's mission in the world. The books in this series are selected to contribute to the development of such wise and humble preachers. The authors represent both scholars of preaching as well as pastors and preachers whose experiences and insights can contribute to passionate and excellent preaching.

OTHER VOLUMES IN THIS SERIES:

The Eloquence of Grace: Joseph Sittler and the Preaching Life edited by James M. Childs Jr. and Richard Lischer

The Preacher as Liturgical Artist: Metaphor, Idenitity, and the Vicarious Humanity of Christ by Trygve David Johnson

Ordinary Preacher, Extraordinary Gospel: A Daily Guide for Wise, Empowered Preachers by Chris Neufeld-Erdman

Bringing Home the Message: How Community Can Multiply the Power of the Preached Word by Robert K. Perkins

Decolonizing Preaching: The Pulpit as Postcolonial Space by Sarah A. N. Travis

Shouting Above
the Noisy Crowd

Biblical Wisdom and the Urgency of Preaching

Essays in Honor of Alyce M. McKenzie

EDITED BY

Charles L. Aaron Jr.
Jaime Clark-Soles

 CASCADE *Books* · Eugene, Oregon

SHOUTING ABOVE THE NOISY CROWD: BIBLICAL WISDOM AND THE
URGENCY OF PREACHING
Essays in Honor of Alyce M. McKenzie

Lloyd John Ogilvie Institute of Preaching Series

Cascade Books
An Imprint of Wipf and Stock Publishers
199 W. 8th Ave., Suite 3
Eugene, OR 97401

www.wipfandstock.com

PAPERBACK ISBN: 978-1-5326-0280-1
HARDCOVER ISBN: 978-1-5326-0282-5
EBOOK ISBN: 978-1-5326-0281-8

Cataloguing-in-Publication data:

Names: Aaron, Charles L., Jr., editor. | Clark-Soles, Jaime, editor.

Title: Shouting above the noisy crowd : biblical wisdom and the urgency of preaching : essays in honor of Alyce M. McKenzie / edited by Charles L. Aaron Jr. and
Jaime Clark-Soles.

Description: Eugene, OR: Cascade Books, 2021 | Series: Lloyd John Ogilvie Institute
of Preaching Series | Includes bibliographical references.

Identifiers: ISBN 978-1-5326-0280-1 (paperback) | ISBN 978-1-5326-0282-5 (hard-
cover) | ISBN 978-1-5326-0281-8 (ebook)

Subjects: LCSH: McKenzie, Alyce M., 1955– | Preaching. | Wisdom—Biblical teach-
ing.

Classification: BS680.W6 S56 2021 (print) | BS680.W6 (ebook)

Contents

Preface

DR. ALYCE MCKENZIE HAS traveled a fascinating path to her influential career in the church and the academy. Following her Master of Divinity from Duke Divinity School in North Carolina, she served as associate pastor at Aldersgate United Methodist Church in York, Pennsylvania. She remembers well the hunger for spiritual nourishment evident in the faces of the people in the pew. Feeding the spiritual hunger of the church has become a defining image of her ministry. Her husband, Murry, encouraged her to pursue a Doctor of Philosophy at Princeton Theological Seminary as a resource for that calling. The couple purchased a home in Pennsylvania near Princeton before the letter of acceptance landed in her mailbox. Feeding spiritual hunger and taking risks have motivated and enabled her ministry along the way.

Prophets thundering at injustice, or Jesus weaving mind-teasing parables stand behind much of the church's understanding of what contemporary preachers do. Following her own path, Alyce has spent much of her life reflecting on the biblical sage as a foundation for preaching. Proverbs, both the book and the genre, offer "freeze-dried scenes." The scenes derive from the observation of life, a practice she describes as the "knack for noticing." These "freeze-dried scenes" await the preacher's insight and skill to expand and enliven the insights tucked into them. The proverb claims a family relationship to the parable, as cousin genres, both of which employ imagination to explore life. Alyce has published in both genres, thus enabling the church to make use of these narratives that reveal, but which require effort and insight to come fully to life.

Besides the potential of the proverb as a brief narrative about life, Alyce recognizes the influence of wisdom on the ministry of Jesus and the church's interpretation of him. She notes the influence of the wisdom tradition and Woman Wisdom herself on the prologue to the Gospel of John. Wisdom provides one of the bridges between the testaments and between the Hebrew Scriptures and the ministry of Jesus. Preachers have tended to neglect the Old Testament and the wisdom literature. With her emphasis on the narrative background of the proverb, the insights into life of the wisdom literature, and her reflection on the influence of wisdom on Jesus, Alyce has made great strides in correcting that neglect.

Alyce has followed the thread of looking for narrative interpretations of life by exploring what preachers can learn from the process of writing novels. Proverbs, parables, and novels all recognize that people are wired to be storytellers. Stories meet people where they are. If twenty-first-century people have short attention spans, narratives pull them in with "palm-sized themes." These "palm-sized themes" enable preachers to "make a scene in the pulpit." Alyce has added another dimension by beginning to explore humor. As she typically does in many situations, Alyce sees the deep potential of humor. Quoting a common chestnut among humor scholars, she declares, "humor is serious business." Preachers should never trivialize the pulpit, but should see the power of humor to lower defenses, heal, and expose what has remained hidden. At a retreat for United Methodist pastors in the North Texas Annual Conference around the turn of the millennium, Alyce wore a jester's cap as part of her presentation. This act summarizes much of what she has done in her career. The jester, portraying the fool, stands in contrast to the sage. Yet the jester, with humor, could speak to the king and mock the king, in ways no one else could.

In a confusing world, people feel hungry for wisdom. Wisdom helps make sense of life. Humor, as one of God's gifts, can challenge the status quo and help people cope. As this introduction takes shape, the world faces a devastating pandemic. Wisdom serves as a tool to limit the damage of this pandemic. Narratives give the human dimension. Humor helps the world survive with sanity intact. Alyce McKenzie has worked to feed the spiritual hunger of the world.

This book began to take shape at a breakfast meeting among Thomas G. Long, John C. Holbert, and Charles Aaron at an Academy of Homiletics meeting in Louisville, Kentucky. The guiding image comes from Prov 1:20–33, where Woman Wisdom cries out in the street. The image connotes strength, power, and the compelling insistence of Woman Wisdom to gain the attention of those who need to hear her word. The image honors the role of wisdom literature in the biblical tradition, and the ministry of Alyce

M. McKenzie. We express gratitude to Professors Long and Holbert, and to the contributors. The book contains both academic chapters and sermons from a variety of scholars and religious leaders. We offer a good mix of established researchers and emerging voices. We submit this volume in the hope that it will enable and persuade the world to heed the cry of Woman Wisdom.

Charles L. Aaron Jr
Jaime Clark-Soles
Biography of Alyce McKenzie
(August 17, 2020)

Biography

The Rev. Dr. Alyce M. McKenzie is George W. and Nell Ayers Le Van Professor of Preaching and Worship at Perkins School of Theology, Southern Methodist University. She joined the faculty at Perkins in 2000. In the spring of 2011 she was named an Altshuler Distinguished Teaching Professor by SMU, the university's highest teaching honor. Dr. McKenzie was the 2012 President of the Academy of Homiletics, an organization of teachers of preaching from North America with a growing international membership. Dr. McKenzie, an ordained United Methodist elder is a member of the North Texas Annual Conference of the United Methodist Church. In 2015, she was the Lyman Beecher Lecturer at Yale Divinity School. These prestigious lectures are the longest-running homiletical lectures in the United States, first begun in 1871.

Dr. McKenzie received her BA in the History of Religions from Bryn Mawr College, her Master of Divinity degree from the Divinity School of Duke University, and her PhD in Theology and Communication in Preaching from Princeton Theological Seminary. She has served churches for twelve years in Pennsylvania, before and during her work on her doctoral degree.

From 1980–88, she served as Associate Pastor at Aldersgate United Methodist Church in York, Pennsylvania. From 1994–98, she served as Visiting Lecturer in Homiletics at Princeton Theological Seminary. While teaching at Princeton Seminary Dr. McKenzie served as interim pastor at Langhorne UMC in Langhorne, Pennsylvania, and Neshamony UMC in Hulmeville, Pennsylvania. From 2012–19, Dr. McKenzie served as "Preacher-in-Residence" at Christ United Methodist Church in Plano, Texas, where she preached regularly and served as preaching coach to members of their clergy staff.

Dr. McKenzie is the Director of the Perkins Center for Preaching Excellence at SMU, a center dedicated to fostering excellence in preaching through innovative workshops and preaching peer groups. One of her passions is helping young preachers gain competence and confidence and young scholars get their research published. She is called on frequently to be guest teacher/preacher at various lay and clergy gatherings and to consult with groups of clergy around the country on creating initiatives to foster preaching excellence.

Dr. McKenzie is the author of ten books and numerous articles, both for scholarly and popular audiences. Her research has focused in the past on preaching the wisdom literature of the Bible: *Preaching Proverbs: Wisdom for the Pulpit* (1996), *The Gospel of Matthew* (1998), *Preaching Biblical Wisdom in a Self-Help Society* (2002), *Hear and Be Wise: Becoming a Teacher and Preacher of Wisdom* (2004), and *The Parables for Today* (2010). Her more recent focus is on the role of the imagination in preaching and on what preachers can learn from novelists and screenwriters: *Novel Preaching: Tips from Top Writers on Crafting Creative Sermons* (2010). In 2011, Dr. McKenzie co-authored a textbook on preaching with Dr. John C. Holbert entitled *What Not to Say: Avoiding the Common Mistakes that Can Sink Your Sermon*. Her most recent book is *Making a Scene in the Pulpit: Vivid Preaching for Visual Listeners*, for which she received SMU's Ford Fellowship Award in 2013. It was published in October of 2018.

Dr. McKenzie's *Wise Up! Four Biblical Virtues for Navigating Life* was published in May 2018 and is being used in small groups and sermon series around the country. She is currently at work on a project, to be co-authored with humor scholar Professor Owen Lynch, entitled *A Funny Thing Happened on the Way to the Pulpit: Preaching and Humor*.

Dr. McKenzie and her husband Murry live in Allen, Texas. They have three grown children: Melissa, Rebecca, and Matthew. They are the doting grandparents of Graham (6) and Silas (2). They are active in First Methodist Church of Allen, where they sing in the Chancel Choir and are members of the Journey Sunday School Class. The McKenzies enjoy travel, musicals, theater, and spending time with friends and family.

PUBLICATIONS

Preaching Proverbs: Wisdom for the Pulpit. Louisville, KY: Westminster John Knox, 1996.
Matthew: Interpretation Bible Studies. Louisville, KY: Westminster John Knox, 2002.
Preaching Biblical Wisdom in a Self-Help Society. Nashville, TN: Abingdon, 2002.

Hear and Be Wise: Becoming a Teacher and Preacher of Wisdom. Nashville, TN: Abingdon, 2004.

Novel Preaching: Fiction Writing Strategies for Sermons. Louisville, KY: Westminster John Knox, 2010.

The Parables for Today. Louisville, KY: Westminster John Knox, 2010.

What Not to Say: Avoiding the Common Mistakes that Can Sink Your Sermon. With John C. Holbert. Louisville, KY: Westminster John Knox, 2011.

Parental Guidance Advised: Adult Preaching from the Old Testament. Co-edited with Charles L. Aaron. St. Louis, MO: Chalice, 2013.

Wise Up! Four Biblical Virtues for Navigating Life. Eugene, OR: Cascade, 2018.

Making a Scene in the Pulpit: Vivid Preaching for Visual Listeners. Louisville, KY: Westminster John Knox, 2018.

Contributors

Charles L. Aaron, Jr., coeditor
Director of the Intern Program
Perkins School of Theology
Southern Methodist University
Dallas, TX

O. Wesley Allen
Lois Craddock Perkins Professor of Homiletics
Perkins School of Theology
Southern Methodist University
Dallas, TX

Jaime Clark-Soles, coeditor
Professor New Testament
Altschuler Distinguished Teaching Professor
Perkins School of Theology
Southern Methodist University
Dallas, TX

Ángel J. Gallardo
Associate Director of the Intern Program
Perkins School of Theology
Southern Methodist University
Dallas, TX

John C. Holbert
Lois Craddock Perkins Professor Emeritus of Homiletics
Perkins School of Theology
Southern Methodist University
Dallas, TX

Ruthanna B. Hooke
Associate Dean of Students and Professor of Homiletics
Virginia Theological Seminar
Alexandria, VA

J. Dwayne Howell
Professor Emeritus of Old Testament and Hebrew
Campbellsville University
Campbellsville, KY

David Schnasa Jacobsen
Bishops Scholar in Homiletics and Preaching
Director Homiletical Theology Project
Boston University School of Theology
Boston, MA

Nancy Kasten
Chief Relationship Officer/Rabbi
Faith Commons
Dallas, TX

Eunjoo Mary Kim
Professor of Homiletics and Liturgics
Iliff School of Theology
Denver, CO

Luke A. Powery
Dean of Duke Chapel
Associate Professor of Homiletics
Duke Divinity School
Duke University
Durham, NC

Carolyn J. Sharp
Professor of Homiletics
Yale Divinity School
Yale University
New Haven, CT

Alma Tinoco Ruiz
Lecturer in Homiletics and Evangelism
Director of the Hispanic House of Studies
Duke Divinity School
Duke University
Durham, NC

Beverly Zink-Sawyer
Professor Emerita of Homiletics
Union Presbyterian Seminary
Richmond, VA

1

Wisdom's Cry and the Task of Preaching

Ruthanna B. Hooke

What does the striking image of Woman Wisdom calling out in the streets in Prov 1:20–21 have to say to preachers about the nature and urgency of the preaching task? Exploration of this question builds on and honors the work of Alyce McKenzie, who has written extensively on models of preaching derived from the wisdom literature in Scripture. McKenzie encourages wisdom preachers to adopt the role of the sage, and to nurture the virtues they extol: reverence for God, attentiveness, self-discipline, and a capacity for subversiveness.[1] She argues that the metaphor of the preacher as sage is particularly suited to our times, in which people are seeking wisdom and often finding it in self-help books and the like, whereas Christian preachers can offer deeper and more sustaining wisdom from the wisdom literature in Scripture, and by modeling themselves after the sages who speak in this literature.

In general, McKenzie derives the characteristics of wisdom preachers from the sages themselves, and the traits they commend in wisdom literature, suggesting that preachers model themselves after these traits. However, she also considers the possibility that contemporary preachers could model themselves after Woman Wisdom herself. She notes that some dismiss Woman Wisdom as a model for preachers, pointing to the fact that

1. McKenzie, *Hear and Be Wise*, xv. See also McKenzie, *Preaching Proverbs*, and McKenzie, *Preaching Biblical Wisdom in a Self-Help Society*.

she speaks only to young men, that she personifies Folly as a woman, and that some of the proverbs attributed to her are misogynist. For these reasons, some consider Woman Wisdom too allied with elitist interests and with the status quo to inform our understanding and practice of preaching. However, McKenzie maintains that there is a subversive element in the metaphor of Woman Wisdom, an element that influenced Jesus and that can continue to influence preachers today.

Building on this suggestion, in this essay I will argue that Woman Wisdom is at her most subversive in her first appearance in Proverbs, in Prov 1:20–33, when she raises her voice in the public square and calls out for followers, condemning in no uncertain terms those who reject her invitation. At this moment in particular, Woman Wisdom disrupts patriarchal culture and its expectations for women's behavior. She uses the fullness of her voice to claim the right to speak in public, breaking taboos both ancient and modern against women's public speech. Not only does she speak in public, but she does so with urgency and prophetic fervor, again rejecting common expectations about what a woman "ought" to sound like. This first utterance of Woman Wisdom offers a galvanizing and empowering image not only for women, but for preachers in general, providing them with a mandate to similarly break taboos against public speech, and to claim a powerful and urgent voice in the public square, as Woman Wisdom does.

I. WOMAN WISDOM: RESONANCES OF THE METAPHOR

In the strongly patriarchal society of ancient Israel, it is surprising that wisdom literature personifies wisdom as female, establishing Woman Wisdom as a central and powerful figure in Proverbs and other wisdom literature. There had to have been significant benefits in this symbolization of wisdom as female to overcome the cultural forces that would have made such a choice unlikely. Claudia Camp investigates the reasons for this choice, exploring the resonance that accrues to the metaphor of Woman Wisdom by virtue of her being female. Camp points out that metaphors work by "conjoin[ing] the semantic field of two words in such a way as to create new meaning."[2] One of the two words is better known than the other, and becomes the "focus" through which the lesser known word, the "frame," is interpreted. In this instance, "woman" is the better known term, through which "wisdom," which is an abstract quality and thus less immediately

2. Camp, *Wisdom and the Feminine in the Book of Proverbs*, 72.

well known, is interpreted. Camp then notes: "To claim that 'woman' is the better known term, however, already begs the question, 'what exactly is it that is known about her?'"[3] Camp's project, then, is to elucidate both the social roles and the literary images attached to women in postexilic Israel, so as to suggest how these roles and images shape the meaning of the term "woman" in the metaphor, through which the idea of "wisdom" is interpreted.

Camp argues that the meaning of the metaphorical relationship between "woman" and "wisdom" derives from the social roles that women filled in postexilic Israel. As the idealized portrait of the "woman of worth" in Prov 31 attests, women functioned as the anchor of the home: they were the house-builders, providers, counselors, hostesses, and the teachers of wisdom to their own children. Their authority was in the domestic sphere, at a time when that domestic sphere was attaining greater importance, with the decline of other societal institutions: "with the collapse of the nation-state, the household became, for the first time in five hundred years, the focus of Israelite identity."[4] The focus on the household shifted a certain amount of societal power to women; women became the glue that held together a society in crisis. As Ellen Davis notes:

> In sum, the woman was to a great extent responsible for maintaining faithful living in Israel. She had assumed many of the mediating, instructional, and guiding functions once performed by the important national figures of priest, prophet, and king. No wonder, then, that when Wisdom came to be personified, it was as a woman, builder and sustainer of the household.[5]

The wisdom tradition sought to stabilize a society in crisis, and did so by personifying Wisdom as a woman, that figure who was a primary stabilizing force in the society itself.

Comparing Woman Wisdom to the social situation of women in postexilic Israel helps the sages describe how wisdom works. For instance, wisdom teaching is grounded in the private and domestic spheres, just as women are in postexilic Israel; their society-sustaining influence goes beyond the home only indirectly. The "woman of worth" in Prov 31 functions predominantly in her home, but her works there are of such quality that they praise her "in the gates." In Prov 9, likewise, Woman Wisdom builds a

---

3. Camp, *Wisdom and the Feminine in the Book of Proverbs*, 74.

4. Davis, *Proverbs, Ecclesiastes, and the Song of Songs*, 17.

5. Davis, *Proverbs, Ecclesiastes, and the Song of Songs*, 18.

house for herself and then invites others into it; she herself does not venture out into the public square, although her invitation does. This depiction of Woman Wisdom as operating chiefly in private domains symbolizes the way that the wisdom tradition exerts its influence: it is not grand, public theology, but rather a set of home truths that speak directly to everyday domestic life, and which only from there indirectly influence the public sphere.

In general, wisdom rules by indirection, in the way women do in patriarchal societies such as ancient Israel. Camp notes that "the exclusion of women (as of any disenfranchised group) from the established hierarchies of authority and power in a society obviously must lead them to utilize less direct means to achieve their goals."[6] She points to various women throughout the Bible who exercise power by indirect means, such as Sarah, Rebekah, Ruth, and Naomi. Taken together, these examples suggest a theological motif of "female initiative on God's behalf by indirect means."[7] In each case, a woman operates without guidance from God, yet achieves God's purposes; moreover, "that purpose accomplished by the women includes the *disruption* of the established hierarchies of society which inhibit both human life and Yahweh's action and the *creation* of a new order of life and freedom for both people and God."[8] Personified Woman Wisdom plays off of these tropes; she too exerts her power by indirection, not by directly influencing human events but by preaching, advising, even manipulating circumstances to achieve God's aims. This indirect influence was credible to postexilic Israel; it "theologically interprets the situation of a politically powerless community."[9] The image of Woman Wisdom working indirectly as God's agent, behind the scenes, to influence events, allowed postexilic Israel to continue believing in Yahweh's power, even when such power was not demonstrably and directly effective in their political reality. The image of Woman Wisdom "effectively mediated the post-exilic community's view of Yahweh's universal rulership in wisdom with their own diminished political stature."[10]

---

6. Camp, *Wisdom and the Feminine in the Book of Proverbs*, 124.

7. Camp, *Wisdom and the Feminine in the Book of Proverbs*, 124.

8. Camp, *Wisdom and the Feminine in the Book of Proverbs*, 125.

9. Camp, *Wisdom and the Feminine in the Book of Proverbs*, 291.

10. Camp, *Wisdom and the Feminine in the Book of Proverbs*, 291.

II. WOMAN WISDOM'S LOUD CRY: DESTABILIZING THE METAPHOR

In exploring the metaphorical comparison of "woman" and "wisdom," Camp demonstrates how this metaphor allowed the sages to depict certain features of how wisdom teaching operates: it stabilizes a society in crisis and lacking strong leaders; its home is the private sphere, and it influences the public sphere only indirectly; and it works through indirect means, which are the means available to the powerless. However, it is intriguing that the behavior of Woman Wisdom in Prov 1:20–33 does not completely fit these attributes of the metaphor. She may be modeled on the social situation of women in ancient Israel, but in her first appearance in Proverbs she breaks the bounds of this social location and its accepted norms. She does not behave in the way that "woman" is supposed to behave. In doing so, she disrupts the terms of the metaphor, generating meanings from it that may not be what the sages themselves intended, but which are particularly valuable for preachers today.

The capacity of the figure of Woman Wisdom to destabilize the metaphor that defines her is inherent in how metaphors work. As Camp notes, the process of interpretation in metaphors is not unidirectional: it is not only the "focus" that interprets the "frame," but the "frame" can also interpret the "focus." The workings of metaphor are such that "even as the lesser known quantity is interpreted through the better known, so also the import of the better known is qualified by the lesser known."[11] The interaction of the two terms generates "a meaning which both partakes of and transforms our understanding of the individual parts."[12] In this instance, then, not only does the better known term, "woman," interpret the lesser known term, "wisdom," but also "wisdom," especially personified Woman Wisdom, reinterprets and transforms the meaning of "woman." There is not a stable, one-to-one correspondence between the two terms of a metaphor; every metaphor threatens to elude the control of those who wield it, generating meanings in the comparison between "focus" and "frame" that are not what the creators of the metaphor intended. Woman Wisdom's public outcry in Prov 1:20–33 is a prime instance of this metaphorical slippage, by which Woman Wisdom transgresses the boundaries of the metaphor, behaving

11. Camp, *Wisdom and the Feminine in the Book of Proverbs*, 73.
12. Camp, *Wisdom and the Feminine in the Book of Proverbs*, 73.

in ways that are outside the norms of women's social location, and, in so doing, subverting those norms.

One way that Woman Wisdom disrupts the metaphor is that, unlike the Israelite woman to whom she is being compared, who remains in the private sphere and influences the public sphere only indirectly, Woman Wisdom in Prov 1:20–33 is unapologetically and assertively public. McKenzie points out that "she is a strong, outspoken woman who shapes the young by the hearth but also leaves home to influence the public arena." Nowhere is her public voice more apparent than in her first appearance in Proverbs:

> Wisdom cries out in the street;
>   in the squares she raises her voice.
> At the busiest corner she cries out;
>   at the entrance of the city gates she speaks. (Prov 1:20–21)[13]

Here Wisdom's behavior is compared to a common practice among teachers, who would go into the public square to compete for students, to declare themselves as possessing the wisdom that students should be seeking. Like these teachers, Wisdom chooses the most central part of the city, the place near the gates where all of the roads fan out around the city, in which to issue her call for students.

In addition to seizing a public voice, Woman Wisdom is exceedingly direct in her first appearance, violating the norms that dictate that women ought to influence matters only indirectly. As soon as she opens her mouth in the most public place in the city, her first words are a rebuke that minces no words: "How long, O simple ones, will you love being simple? . . . Because I have called and you refused,/have stretched out my hand and no one heeded . . . I also will laugh at your calamity . . ." (Prov 1:22, 24, 26). She condemns and judges those who do not listen to her: "because they hated knowledge and did not choose the fear of the Lord,/would have none of my council and despised all of my reproof,/therefore they shall eat the fruit of their way . . . For waywardness kills the simple, and the complacency of fools destroys them" (Prov 1:29–32a). There is nothing indirect or demure in this warning and condemnation; indeed, Woman Wisdom's words here echo those of the prophets, who likewise warned of God's judgment on those who would not heed their warnings, and promised that to disregard their words was to choose the path leading to destruction. Here, too, in

---

13. All Scripture quotations are from the New Revised Standard Version unless noted otherwise.

adopting a form of speech that is direct, condemnatory, and full of judgment, Woman Wisdom is not behaving in a traditionally womanly manner.

Furthermore, Woman Wisdom's claiming prophetic speech undermines her supposed role as a stabilizing agent in society. The Israelite prophets, although they were calling the people back to their original covenant with God, often functioned to disrupt a complacent society that had fallen away from that covenant. So Amos added a condemnation of the people of Israel along with his condemnation of foreign nations, and Jeremiah inveighed against the false prophets who proclaimed "Peace, peace, when there is no peace," and the complacent populace who were all too willing to believe them, instead of facing into the crisis that was at their doorstep (Jer 6:14). Woman Wisdom, in taking on the prophetic voice in Prov 1:20–33, echoes the voice of the prophets, who do not seek to stabilize or comfort their society, but to disrupt, challenge, and warn it. In claiming this voice, Woman Wisdom departs from the normative womanly role of stabilizing the society.

One indication that Woman Wisdom's calling out loudly in the public square is ambiguous and potentially scandalous, not in keeping with woman's appropriate conduct, is that this same behavior is also attributed to the "foolish woman" or the "strange woman." Throughout Prov 1–9, Woman Wisdom's behavior is contrasted with this archetypically dangerous woman, who seeks out young men only to waylay them into adultery and folly. Interestingly, however, this perilous woman acts exactly like Woman Wisdom in seeking to carry out her nefarious intention. The strange woman, too, is "loud," and like Woman Wisdom, she "does not stay at home;/ now in the street, now in the squares, and at every corner she lies in wait" (Prov 7:11–12). Later this "foolish woman" is described as "loud," and like Woman Wisdom "she sits at the door of her house, on a seat at the high places of the town, calling to those who pass by . . . 'You who are simple, turn in here'" (Prov 9:14–16a). One effect of this close similarity between the behaviors of Woman Wisdom and the "strange woman" is to make the point that to seek wisdom is always a dangerous and ambiguous enterprise, that sometimes it is hard to distinguish between wisdom and folly, and it is easy to be led astray by forces that seem like wisdom but are not. However, another effect of this close similarity is to heighten the hint of scandal in Woman Wisdom's behavior. By going to the most public places to call out for students, she is acting in a way that is, in general, unacceptable for Israelite women, since aside from Woman Wisdom herself, the only other women who behave as she does are prostitutes and foolish women. There is a hint of taboo-breaking in her behavior, a sign that the metaphor of Woman Wisdom is becoming unruly. It no longer reinforces women's traditional roles, but subverts them, suggesting a previously unheard-of public role for women's speaking.

III. WOMAN'S PUBLIC SPEECH: BREAKING A TABOO

One reason that the image of Woman Wisdom crying out in public feels incongruous and even scandalous is because the taboos it challenges are prevalent not only in ancient Israelite society, but in Western culture more universally. Taboos that forbid women's public speech are deeply embedded in the Western cultural imaginary. Classicist Mary Beard notes that the prohibition against women's public speech is present as far back as Homer's *Odyssey,* in which Odysseus's son, Telemachus, silences his mother in front of a crowd, telling her to "go back up into your quarters, and take up your own work, the loom and the distaff . . . speech will be the business of men, all men, and of me most of all; for mine is the power in this household."[14] As Beard points out, this silencing of his mother is one of the crucial moments in Telemachus's passage to manhood; to become a man, then, is in part to "take control of public utterance," and to silence women who want to take part in such speech. It is telling, says Beard, that this incident occurs in some of the earliest written examples of Western culture. Beard adduces many other examples in ancient Greco-Roman culture of women being silenced, all of which prove that:

> Public speaking and oratory were not merely things that ancient women *didn't do*: they were exclusive practices and skills that defined masculinity as a gender. As we saw with Telemachus, to become a man (or at least an elite man) was to claim the right to speak. Public speech was a—if not *the*—defining attribute of maleness. Or, to quote a well-known Roman slogan, the elite male citizen could be summed up as *vir bonus dicendi peritus,* 'a good man, skilled in public speaking.' A woman speaking in public was, in most circumstances, by definition not a woman.[15]

Within the Christian canon, the silencing of women is a notable theme, as for instance in Paul's directive to the Corinthians: "women should be

14. Beard, *Women and Power*, 4.
15. Beard, *Women and Power*, 17.

silent in the churches. For they are not permitted to speak, but should be subordinate, as the law also says. If there is anything they desire to know, let them ask their husbands at home. For it is shameful for a woman to speak in church" (1 Cor 14:34–35). Women have often been punished for breaking this command, as for instance the early Methodist preacher Madame Perrott, who "preached the word of life to all who would hear, in private houses, both in town and country, and while thus engaged she was sometimes pelted with mud, and otherwise very roughly and cruelly treated."[16]

Beard maintains that the exclusion of women from public speech continues to this day, pointing to the abuse she herself has received for her forthright public speaking, and the recent silencing of Senator Elizabeth Warren on the US Senate floor. Beard also points out that some of these criticisms attach to the sound of the female voice itself, which is accused of being "strident" or "whiny," as compared to the "deep" and automatically authoritative male voice. So strong is this prejudice that Margaret Thatcher took voice lessons to lower her voice so that it would sound more manly, hence authoritative; conversely, many of the lines of attack against Hillary Clinton, during her 2012 and 2016 presidential campaigns, focused on the sound of her voice. As Beard notes, "It is still the case that when listeners hear a female voice, they do not hear a voice that connotes authority; or rather they have not learned how to hear authority in it."[17] Nancy Lammers Gross, in her recent work on women's voices in preaching, confirms that prejudices against women preaching are still very much alive and well.[18]

IV. WOMAN WISDOM'S CALL TO PREACHERS

Given these prohibitions, ancient and modern, against women's public speech, the image of Woman Wisdom calling out boldly in the public square is daring and incongruous, even for contemporary readers. In her taboo-breaking behavior, Woman Wisdom offers a model of liberating speech and action that can empower not only women but all who would break taboos in order to speak God's word boldly and in public spaces. Woman Wisdom has had this effect at various points in Christian history, empowering later preachers who draw from her example, including Jesus of Nazareth. Elisabeth Schüssler Fiorenza argues that the earliest strand of the Jesus tradition,

16. McKenzie, *Hear and Be Wise*, 167.

17. Beard, *Women and Power*, 30.

18. Gross, *Women's Voices and the Practice of Preaching*, 42–73.

and quite possibly Jesus's own self-understanding, is that he was Wisdom's prophet.[19] As a spokesperson for Woman Wisdom, Jesus authorized and created space for the public speaking of women, a practice that is evident in the Gospels and earliest Pauline Epistles, but was suppressed after the first flowering of the church, as Paul's prohibitions indicate. In addition, Jesus as a delegate of Woman Wisdom continues her subversive work, for instance in his proclamation of release to the captives and good news to the poor.

In addition to empowering Jesus's subversive work, and the public speech of women in the early church, Woman Wisdom seems to have authorized the public speech of women at other points in Christian history. Perhaps the preaching of Methodist preacher Madame Perrott was emboldened by the image of Woman Wisdom's public proclamation. Perhaps, too, John Wesley's encouragement of a woman preacher was an exhortation to follow the example of Woman Wisdom: "If you speak only faintly and indirectly, none will be offended and none profited. But if you speak out, although some will probably be angry, yet others will soon find the power of God unto salvation."[20]

Although Woman Wisdom's loud and direct public speech has inspired earlier generations of Christian preachers, there are liberating possibilities in this image that preachers have yet to actualize. Schüssler Fiorenza argues that her work tracing Divine Sophia's influence on Jesus of Nazareth is so that "the theological possibilities offered by Wisdom, the Divine Woman of Justice, but never quite realized in history, can be realized."[21] There are several ways in which preachers can claim Woman Wisdom as a model, and so work toward realizing the possibilities in this image.

The very fact that Woman Wisdom speaks in the public square, violating taboos in her own culture as well as prohibitions lodged deeply in the Western cultural imagination, can empower not only women, but all who have been silenced, to claim their voices in public. The image provides authorization for preachers to speak and to claim public space even if they are "supposed" to remain silent and private. As Ellen Davis notes, Woman Wisdom risks public contempt in order to speak for God.[22] Preachers can emulate Woman Wisdom's example and do the same, even at the risk of similarly enduring contempt. The example of Woman Wisdom helps in bearing this reaction, since the scandal of Woman Wisdom's public speech

19. Schüssler Fiorenza, *Jesus*, 139.

20. John Wesley, quoted in McKenzie, *Hear and Be Wise*, 168.

21. Schüssler Fiorenza, *Jesus*, 133.

22. Davis, *Proverbs, Ecclesiastes, and the Song of Songs*, 34.

can remind those whose public voice is forbidden that when they break silence, they too are breaking a powerful taboo. Understanding this allows these speakers to expect resistance to their speaking, so that they are not defeated by this resistance, but instead persist through it.

The image of Woman Wisdom calling out in the public square also summons preachers to reclaim a public voice. Against the tendency to believe that Christian proclamation and witness ought to be limited to the private and personal spheres, the depiction of Woman Wisdom claiming space and voice in the busiest part of the city offers preachers a counterexample. Like her, Christian preachers are summoned to enter into the busiest places of our common life and to demand attention for their proclamation of the Christian witness. As Woman Wisdom had to compete for attention and call out for followers amidst a throng of other teachers proclaiming other paths, so too the contemporary preacher is competing for attention with a range of other paths and truths in an increasingly pluralist and secular society. The figure of Woman Wisdom encourages preachers in post-Christian societies not to shrink from this challenge, but to embrace it boldly.

One reason to embrace this challenge is that the stakes are high, and this, too, the preacher can learn from Woman Wisdom's public proclamation. There is urgency in her summons to the way of wisdom. She offers a dire warning to the fools and scoffers who ignore her call, echoing the prophets in declaring that those who do not follow her will be "destroyed" in their "complacency" (Prov 1:32).Wisdom's call is to come to understand life so as to live it well, exercising the virtues of prudence, understanding, and self-control. Woman Wisdom's proclamation in Prov 1:20–33 is that, if we do not do this, we choose the way of ruin. Preachers likewise need to convey this urgency in their proclamation, a sense that choosing to live by wisdom's virtues is a matter of ultimate importance, and to reject the way of wisdom is to choose the path of destruction. Woman Wisdom shows how preachers can emulate virtues from the wisdom tradition, while at the same time harnessing the power of the prophetic voice.

Preachers can express this synthesis between the wisdom tradition and the prophetic on many topics, but one situation that clearly invites a synthesis of the wisdom tradition with the urgency of the prophetic is our relationship with the rest of creation. The wisdom tradition places a high value on living in harmony with creation. Wisdom literature celebrates the wondrous order of creation, and points to divine wisdom undergirding that order, paradigmatically in Woman Wisdom's presence as a master worker assisting God in creating the world. Human wisdom, as Ellen Davis points out, "consists in observing the created order, learning from it, living in ways that do not violate—indeed, that contribute—to the well-being of the whole created order."[23] In a time of environmental crisis, when the human relationship to creation is particularly unhealthy, this emphasis of the wisdom tradition demands to be proclaimed, urgently and publicly, following the example of Woman Wisdom.

V. THE RAISED VOICE AND THE RINGING CRY

Harnessing the power in the image of Woman Wisdom speaking in the public square has to do with emulating her way of speaking, and the power of her voice. It is striking that Woman Wisdom is described as "crying out" and "raising her voice" (Prov 1:20). The verb in this verse suggests a "ringing tone," a "fervent, piercing cry," which elsewhere in the Bible is used in moments of great joy or distress.[24] Woman Wisdom is using her physical voice in its fullest power and expressiveness, which preachers need to learn how to do as well, since many preachers do not have access to the full freedom and power of their physical voices.

The process of discovering and using the free voice requires an understanding of how the voice works, and why it often does not work as well as it can. When the voice is working optimally, speaking begins with the desire to communicate, which stimulates breathing muscles—abdominal muscles, diaphragm, and rib muscles—and they expand to let breath in. The breath supports the sound, which is amplified by all of the resonators in the body. The voice, when working properly, is connected to the body and to the selfhood of the speaker, and it can communicate the full range of her thought and feeling. However, this natural process is often curtailed, especially in those who have been denied the right to speak. Such speakers learn that it is not socially acceptable to express the full range of their thought and feeling with passion. Such social conditioning leads speakers to detach their impulse to communicate from the diaphragm and abdominal muscles, the source of the voice's power and freedom, and to express that impulse through the throat and face. The voice becomes disconnected from the body, unsupported by the breath, and is squeezed out by overworking the throat, jaw, and tongue muscles. Such speaking leads to the divorce of words from meaning and emotion, the disconnection of the speaker from

23. Davis, *Proverbs, Ecclesiastes, and the Song of Songs*, 5.
24. Davis, *Proverbs, Ecclesiastes, and the Song of Songs*, 33.

her words. In addition, the voice itself often becomes strident, nasal, or whiny, because it is fueled by tension rather than by the freedom of breath connected to thought and feeling.

This is the situation in which many women, and others who lack the societal power or authorization to speak, find themselves. Laboring under the taboos against public speech, and against speech that conveys their true passion, many have learned to curtail the full freedom of their voice. They have learned to accommodate their voices to the demands of others and to cultural notions of what is acceptable speech. To compound the problem, this very lack of freedom in their voices may contribute to distortions in the voice, such as stridency or nasality, which makes them that much more difficult to listen to and hear. For this reason the complaints about the sound of women's voices are doubly problematic, since they blame women for distortions that were brought about by the unwillingness to listen to women in the first place.

In the face of all these obstacles to speaking, the loud and ringing sound of Woman Wisdom's voice can summon preachers, especially those denied the right to speak, to reclaim this full and free voice. There are physical steps that can be undertaken in order to do this; the Linklater method, for instance, takes students through a progression of physical and vocal exercises that are designed to free and strengthen the speaking voice by reconnecting speakers' voices to their bodies and emotions.[25] The goal of the method is fully embodied communication, in which the voice and body are free, in which the words spoken do not exist only in the mind but are connected to and expressed through the whole body. When we speak with this freedom, there is a deeper sense of personal presence and authority, as well as a stronger connection to the meaning of the words spoken, and to the hearers.

I use an exercise in my preaching classes that aims to replicate Woman Wisdom's use of the free voice to claim attention in the busy public square. If a student preaches a sermon that is too hesitant, casual, or demure, I ask the entire class to start walking around the classroom space, talking to each other, checking their phones, distracted by whatever is going on in their minds. The task of the preacher is to preach her sermon in such a way that she gets the attention of her classmates, compelling them to leave off whatever they are focused on so as to pay attention to her. This exercise requires the preacher to claim her authority, her right to speak and be heard, and to

25. This voice method is outlined in Linklater, *Freeing the Natural Voice.*

confront those voices, internal and external, that tell her to be quiet. To do this, she needs to discover the urgent desire to communicate her message, a desire that is somewhere deep within her. Then she needs to let this passion find its way into her voice, so that, like Woman Wisdom, she speaks in a ringing voice which cannot be ignored or silenced.

To reconnect with the power of the voice requires the courage to acknowledge the truths our bodies know, and the courage to speak these truths, confronting the cultural taboos that demand our silence. This courage ultimately goes beyond our human capacity, and can only be grounded in our relationship with God. Here, too, Woman Wisdom helps the preacher, since she is an agent or aspect of God, through whom God's gracious presence is accessible. The effect of personifying wisdom is that wisdom teaching is not merely an abstract set of precepts, but a person whom one can love and follow, and from whom one can seek help. Not only does Woman Wisdom cry out to the student, but the student can cry out to her. Shortly after Woman Wisdom's prophetic speech in Prov 1, the sage addresses the student of wisdom and urges him to "cry out for insight,/and raise your voice for understanding" (Prov 2:3). If he does so, he will "understand the fear of the Lord, and find the knowledge of God" (Prov 2:5). The verbs used for "crying out" and "raising your voice" are the same used for Woman Wisdom's public address in Prov 1:20. This parallel suggests that preachers who seek to echo Woman Wisdom's proclamation can gain strength for doing so from Woman Wisdom herself. Before preachers cry out in public, they need to cry out to her for insight and guidance. Woman Wisdom can then become a divine source of guidance for those who seek to emulate her daring, urgent, and subversive public preaching.

2

When Worldviews Collide

J. Dwayne Howell

We are confronted in the news with ideas of alternative facts, "fake news," and calls to not believe what we see or hear. In an almost Orwellian fashion we are told the truth is not the truth. This divisiveness has entered into our congregations, with differing worldviews unwilling to yield to each other. Why do we so stubbornly hold on to our opinions and beliefs? Why are there such divergent points of view on what is and what is not truth, and how are ministers to address this truth crisis? A reading of Proverbs and an understanding of the development of worldviews can provide some insight into this phenomenon.

Proverbs is classified as practical wisdom, wisdom that provides guidance for daily living.[1] Such wisdom regularly provides a dichotomy between right and wrong choices for life. For Proverbs, wisdom is found in understanding the divine order that is present in creation. The order reflects God's creative and sustaining work in the world, and the wise live within that order. To oppose such order leads to chaos. For the writers of Proverbs those who choose to live in chaos are called fools. Fools can be seen as a derogatory term today and might not aid in bringing about peace between differing views. Actually, the writers of Proverbs use several terms to describe those who live at odds with the divine order. The two primary

1. Alyce M. McKenzie has written on preaching from Proverbs in *Hear and Be Wise: Becoming a Preacher and Teacher of Wisdom.*

words are *elim* and *kesil*, often translated as "fool" or "folly," are frequently used in Proverbs to contrast the wise with the imprudent. Another common term is the simpleton (*peti*) who is easily swayed from one view to another without firmly holding to any particular view. *Nabal* is used only twice in Proverbs and refers to a brutish type of character (17:7; 30:32).

One word in particular, *lets* ("mocker"), describes one stubbornly set in his or her ways, unwilling to change even in the face of contradicting facts.[2] It is a verb form used sixteen times in Proverbs, most often as a participle (14x—translated like a noun and commonly used in the plural, *letsym*, "mockers"). It is the same plural participle found in Ps 1 where the righteous person does not sit with the "mockers" (1:1). Prov 21:24 defines *lets* as: "The proud and arrogant person—"Mocker" is his name—behaves with insolent fury." Alyce M. McKenzie rightly observes "The *lutz* (sic) is a know-it-all unteachable person."[3]

Proverbs does not regard mockers in high esteem because of the disturbance they create within the community. Mockery, when not used in reference to a person, is equated with the inebriation of wine elsewhere (20:1). The reader is first introduced to the mockers in Prov 1:22, where they are included in a list of other types of offenders:

> 22 "How long will you who are simple love your simple ways?
> How long will mockers delight in mockery
> and fools hate knowledge?

This passage is part of Wisdom's call for these people to learn from Wisdom and turn from their wayward ways. However, Wisdom has little hope of persuading them and "mocks" (v. 26) them in their ruin (vv. 24–32). For the writers of Proverbs, judgment will be brought upon the mockers by God (3:34; 19:29). Little hope is held out for the wayward in Proverbs.

There is a futility in trying to convince mockers to change their ways. First, they will not listen:

> A wise son heeds his father's instruction,
> but a mocker does not respond to rebukes. (13:1)

> Mockers resent correction,
> so they avoid the wise. (15:12)

---

2. I will use the NIV translation and its definition of the *les* as "mocker" throughout the paper.

3. McKenzie, *Hear and Be Wise*, 8. Gerhard von Rad defined *les* as "unrestrained boastful behavior" (*Wisdom in Israel*, 65).

Trying to convince mockers of their mistaken beliefs or obstinate attitude will only lead to making matters worse. A key difference between the wise and the mocker is that the wise are willing to learn and show appreciation for correction. However, the mockers refuse to be corrected and turn away from those offering help.

> 7 Whoever corrects a mocker invites insults;
> whoever rebukes the wicked incurs abuse.
> 8 Do not rebuke mockers or they will hate you;
> rebuke the wise and they will love you.
> 12 If you are wise, your wisdom will reward you;
> if you are a mocker, you alone will suffer.
> (9:7–8, 12; cf. 14:6)

Mockers are associated with evil in the Sayings of the Wise (22:17—24:22).

> 8 Whoever plots evil
> will be known as a schemer.
> 9 The schemes of folly are sin,
> and people detest a mocker. (24:8–9, Saying 24)

McKenzie observes that the mocker's "supercilious arrogance sets the whole community on edge."[4] Because of the discord that they can cause in the congregation, Proverbs encourages the community to drive them out in order to find peace (22:10).[5] They are likewise destined for punishment (19:29). The writers believe that in punishing the mockers it might provide teaching moments for the simple-minded in the community (19:25; 21:11).

Perhaps the descriptions of the mocker found in Proverbs brings to mind particular persons in one's life or even one's own actions. Why can people be so obstinate? One reason is how we see the world around us. As we have life experiences we develop a worldview that is shaped by those experiences. The experiences serve as a reminder of what we have learned and what has happened in our lives in the past and helps us make future decisions by taking those experiences and constructing them into personal worldviews.[6] For example, when we come to the Bible we do not come to

4. McKenzie, Hear and Be Wise, 8.

5. Clifford, Proverbs, 197. Clifford sees this as being a public assembly: "If one expels a scornful person from a meeting, hateful and unproductive attitudes are gotten rid of also. Wherever scoffers, who are contemptuous of others (21:24), set the tone there will be no harmony."

6. The concept of building a worldview on one's life experiences is based on the

it with a blank slate. Instead, we bring all of our experiences to reading the text. These experiences can include our cultural setting, educational background, religious upbringing, and even our own prejudices. All these and other factors affect our interpretation of Scripture. The same can be said about other aspects important to our lives, including politics. Because everyone has different life experiences, we develop different worldviews and at times these worldviews come into conflict. Such conflict often challenges one's basis of belief and the response to differing information is frequently resistance.[7] It is easier to accept information that adds to one's beliefs than information that may challenge them. The propensity to only accept positive or affirming information is called "confirmation bias."

A variety of factors are found in the development of confirmation bias. The following examples are intended to provided insight into confirmation bias and should not be considered a comprehensive list. A first factor to consider is what one uses for sources of information. With the rise of social media today, stories, without regard to accuracy, spread faster than ever before. People tend to follow sources that support their own perspective regardless of the veracity of the material.[8] In a recent study published in the journal *Science*, researchers reviewed 3 million tweets on Twitter between 2006 and 2016. Using six independent fact-checking organizations, the study found that: "Falsehood diffused significantly farther, faster, deeper, and more broadly than the truth in all categories of information and the effects were more pronounced for false political news than for false news about terrorism, natural disasters, science, urban legends, or financial information."[9] Social media readily provides a place for conspiracy theories, hate rhetoric, and dubious facts. However, many will accept the information as factual when developing their worldview.[10] Added to the rise of social media are two additional aspects: The 24-hour news cycle and

concept of "Construct Theory." Originally used in psychology, it is now used in various disciplines. A proctored site with information about Construct theory can be found at: http://www.pcp-net.org/encyclopaedia/main.html.

7. Once one's worldview is set, it is often hard to change even with countering facts. See Kolbert, "Why Facts Don't Change Our Minds"; Keohane, "How Facts Backfire"; and Funkhouser, "Willing Belief and the Norm of Truth."

8. Pierre, "Fake News, Echo Chambers & Filter Bubbles."

9. Vosoughi, "Spread of True and False News Online," 1146.

10. Heath et al., "How a Lie Took Hold and Took Off." This is a story about how social media played a role in the mass shootings in a Pittsburgh, Pennsylvania synagogue on October 28, 2018.

the decline of print journalism. With the rise of the 24-hour news cycles programs have developed differing perspectives on current events, often catering to specific demographics. The decline of print journalism is due in part to decreasing revenue, leading newspapers and magazines to either close or greatly reduce their staffs. These reductions have limited journalism's ability to do in-depth research on key topics.

A second factor in the development of confirmation bias is the way in which a research methodology is chosen and interpreted when developing a hypothesis. Sometimes, whether intentional or not, it can tilt the research to certain outcomes. In his article, "Varieties of Confirmation Bias," Joshua Klayman list several reasons for bias in research.[11] First, *a person may begin overconfident in the initial belief.* Such arrogance can blind one to any variation in the research. Secondly, a person may *search for evidence in a way that biases the data to favor the hypothesis.* This includes the avoidance of any type of research that may disprove the hypothesis. Third, the *interpretation of the information might be biased in favor of the hypothesis.* Information is malleable and can be made to fit a variety of perspectives. Surveys or public information can be shaped in such a way to support a preplanned outcome. Fourth, *revision of one's confidence in the hypothesis may be insufficient given one's beliefs about the strength of the data.* While discrepancies may be noted, their full implication on the research may be ignored. Finally, there may be *trouble generating viable new hypotheses even when in doubt about the old one.* One may simply give up on his or her hypothesis, seeing it difficult to accept an alternative hypothesis.

Another factor that leads to confirmation bias is found in the groups with which one associates. People are often attracted to like-minded people. They often share common backgrounds, experiences, and beliefs. While this may happen within the church, it can also happen in other social structures including work, recreation, family, or political affiliation. Even the academy is not immune from groups of differing opinions. In their article, "Diagnosing Bias in Philosophy and Religion," Paul Draper and Ryan Draper speak to the partisanship found in the Philosophy of Religion discipline.[12] "Unsurprisingly, in the case of confirmation bias, it was found for all groups examined that proponents of an issue sought out more *supporting* than *opposing* arguments."[13] One significant point of their article is

---

11. Klayman, "Varieties of Confirmation Bias," 386–87.

12. Draper and Nichols, "Diagnosing Bias in Philosophy of Religion."

13. Draper and Nichols, "Diagnosing Bias in Philosophy of Religion," 426.

that many in the group did not realize that they were using confirmation bias, stating that it often operates on an unconscious level.[14]

All people are susceptible to bias in decision-making, especially if it challenges their developed worldviews. However, true learning comes from challenging and refining our current beliefs. Within the Wisdom literature is also found speculative wisdom which challenges the right and wrong dichotomy of practical wisdom. Books such as Job and Ecclesiastes directly question the black-and-white world presented in practical wisdom and its simple answers. Life is messy and there are at times no simple answers to complex issues. Job's friends, Eliphaz, Bildad, and Zophar, show that practical wisdom can be abused when dealing with others. These "friends" try to comfort and correct Job in his suffering using practical wisdom. However, they fail and in the end are punished for their behavior (Job 42:7–9). True wisdom comes in not simply knowing and quoting wisdom, but in knowing how to appropriately apply wisdom to life. McKenzie reminds us: "In our teaching and preaching, it is important to acknowledge our own tendencies toward folly and the chaos it brings, but also to celebrate the progress we have made on the path of wisdom."[15] It is easy to believe that we have all the answers, but as the seventies' song reminds us, "Everybody plays the fool, sometime."[16]

We live in a world of different perspectives on how the world operates. Often these worldviews collide and tensions arise. We cannot control how others will respond to us. However, we can control how we respond to others. Prov 9:12 emphasizes the choice we can make for ourselves: "If you are wise, your wisdom will reward you; if you are a mocker, you alone will suffer." The following are some suggestions on how to deal with personal bias in the development of our own worldviews.

1) Humility—We do not know everything and are limited by our own personal experiences of the world around us. Humility does not mean subservience to others. It involves developing a proper perspective of our own self-understanding while also acknowledging that others are worthy of our attention and that we may learn from them as well. McKenzie states: "The sages' goal amid a society marred by temptation and corruption, was to instill in the young the qualities of character

14. Draper and Nichols, "Diagnosing Bias in Philosophy of Religion," 435.

15. McKenzie, *Hear and Be Wise*, 8.

16. The Main Ingredient, "Everybody Plays the Fool." Full lyrics at: https://genius.com/The-main-ingredient-everybody-plays-the-fool-lyrics.

that make for harmony in both personal and public life: deference to God's guidance as the giver of wisdom, moderation and self-control, and compassion for the less fortunate."[17]

2) Openness to learning—Learning is a lifelong process. New information and perspectives are constantly challenging one's worldview. In learning, it is beneficial to study other information that is contrary to one's own beliefs. This helps not only to see the strengths and weaknesses of other positions, but can also help to expose weaknesses in one's own presuppositions.

3) Ability to listen—It is important to develop dialogue with others. Too often disagreements digress into a one-way monologue with those who have differing opinions. Dialogue requires the ability to listen to the other as well as to respond appropriately. One way to have open discussions with others is through planned sermon topics. John McClure outlines such "round-table" discussions in his book, *The Round-Table Pulpit*.[18]

4) Verify, verify, verify!—It is of utmost importance in sermon research and preparation that all information is accurate and from sound sources. Interpretations of current events need to be substantiated by using a variety of sources. While the internet can provide quick information, some of the information has not been properly vetted. When studying information, it is best if it is peer-reviewed by competent people in the field of study. Illustrations, quotes, and statistics need to be confirmed by referring to primary sources. If facts have to be distorted to get a message across, is it a message that needs to be shared?

5) Know when to walk away. There are times when one or both sides are not willing to listen or to learn from one another, making any continued discussion an exercise in futility. Those who seek to maintain intolerant, hate-filled ideas also need to be avoided. As the writer of Proverbs reminds us, to continue such discussions only serves to make an enemy (Prov 9:8). Knowing when to disengage a discussion can sometimes be the better part of valor.

17. McKenzie, *Hear and Be Wise*, 8–9.
18. McClure, *Round-Table Pulpit*.

3

Is Preaching Political?

Luke A. Powery

> *Is not this the fast that I choose:*
> *to loose the bonds of injustice,*
> *to undo the thongs of the yoke,*
> *to let the oppressed go free,*
> *and to break every yoke?*
> *Is it not to share your bread with the hungry,*
> *and bring the homeless poor into your house;*
> *when you see the naked, to cover them,*
> *and not to hide yourself from your own kin?*
> —Isa 58:6–7

INTRODUCTION

THE OPENING SCRIPTURAL EPIGRAPH reveals a broadening of the traditional understanding of the spiritual practice of fasting. In fact, it is a reimagination of fasting, away from a private act to a public one, even a political one. Fasting, in this setting, is no longer abstention from food, nor is it, in the case of the people in this passage, abstention from just treatment of people. Rather, fasting is righteous public engagement with the oppressed. In other words, fasting, worship, is a political act. God speaks through the prophet Isaiah and aligns practices with the political realm and the everyday world.

God speaks and integrates worship and social witness. This Scripture implicitly affirms what Rafael Avila wrote, "The apolitical nature of the church is an ideological illusion."[1]

Fast-forward closer to our day and the Rev. Dr. Martin Luther King Jr. during the Civil Rights movement, and one can easily observe that there was no illusion about the church being apolitical. King was motivated to engage the public square out of his understanding of the gospel and the role of the church in the world. Not surprisingly, there were other views and approaches contrary to his, even within the church. It is true that "there is more than one way to relate religion and culture"[2] but they *have* to be related to one another in light of the gospel of Jesus Christ. The perpetual question is, "How?"

The tension then and now about how the church should be engaged in the political realm is clearly revealed in King's 1963 "Letter from the Birmingham Jail." In it, he articulates the tension within Christian circles about engagement with societal issues. He writes, "In the midst of a mighty struggle to rid our nation of racial and economic injustice, I have heard many ministers say: 'Those are social issues with which the gospel has no real concerns.' And I have watched many churches commit themselves to a completely other-worldly religion which makes a strange, un-Biblical distinction between body and soul, between the sacred and the secular . . ."[3]

This historical struggle over the relationship between the gospel and society or the public realm or politics is past, present, and will be ongoing into the future. The ecclesial tensions over this relationship still exist and can be heard when a preacher is told: "Just preach the gospel. Stay out of politics!" As this statement echoes around the sanctuaries of the church, this essay will attempt to engage its sound by exploring the relationship between preaching and politics and posing the question, "Is preaching political?"

Through an exploration of the meaning of "political," the divine gesture of incarnation, and the nature of the gospel, it will become evident that the theo-rhetorical practice of preaching is political. In other words, if one is preaching the gospel of Jesus Christ, it is impossible to be apolitical because the gospel is inherently political.

---

1. Avila, *Worship and Politics*, 189.

2. Volf, *Public Faith*, xiv.

3. King, "Letter from a Birmingham Jail," para. 29.

MEANING OF "POLITICAL"

Often, the church struggles with what is meant by "political" or "politics." When that term is sometimes used on Christian tongues, it is meant to be derogatory ("Stay out of politics!"). However, when we consider the root meaning of the word—political—it is impossible to stay out of it. If we live in the world, we are engaged in the political. Embedded in the word political is the word, *polis*, which is the historical term referring to an ancient Greek city-state. *Polis* is the broader society in which we live, move, and have our being. The police work in the *polis*, our society. Thus, when using the word "political" for this essay and for my own homiletical framework, it refers to public affairs and engagement with our society and world. Political does not mean party politics or partisanship within the context of a United States democracy or governmental political system.

The political, in the way I describe, is inescapable. We are *in* the world, a political world. We are political creatures just by the nature of being humans on the earth. Christian ethicist and theologian Stanley Hauerwas writes, "There is no escaping 'the political.' To refuse to take a political stance is to take a political stance. In particular, the presumption that the church is above politics underwrites the distinction between the public and the private that serves to relegate strong convictions, particularly if they are 'religious,' to the private."[4] Hauerwas points to the impossibility of apoliticality. To be political is to be engaged with and attuned to the public life, the enfleshed life. Framing "the political" in this way opens up fruitful conversation with theology and the way God engages politics in God's own being through the incarnation.

INCARNATION AS GOD'S POLITICAL ACT

The incarnation of God in Jesus Christ was God's political act or political sermon in that God entered the sphere of public human affairs. God entered the political realm, in the way defined above, through the incarnation. God "preached" this Word "[i]n those days [when] a decree went out from Emperor Augustus that all the world should be registered. This was the first registration and was taken while Quirinius was governor of Syria" (Luke 2:1–2). In the Gospel of Matthew, the coming of Christ into the world happened "in the time of King Herod . . . " (Matt 2:1). God in

---

4. "Do Politics Belong in Church?," para. 41.

Christ entered the political world. Even for God, politics was unavoidable and because God interjected God's word into this realm, everyone was not happy. Certain people, like the power brokers of the day such as King Herod, thought God should stay out of politics and stay out of their way. Herod was frightened and threatened by this new child king in town and sought to kill him. From the very beginning, God made a political statement through the incarnation.

"In the beginning was the Word, and the Word was with God, and the Word was God. He was in the beginning with God . . . And the Word became flesh and lived among us . . . " (John 1:1–14). God became human in this world and did not distance himself from public human affairs. Christ lived in communities, among the people, in the everydayness of human political reality. He experienced the good, the bad, and the ugly of public life. The incarnation reminds us that preaching is not solely *Logos*, a divine Word, but is also a human Word because God is interested in human affairs in public, that is, politics. God's Word touches the earth, society, and politics.

It is important to begin this conversation about preaching and politics with the incarnate Word of God because faith's relationship to the broader world and culture should be "defined by the center of the faith itself, by its relation to Christ as the divine Word incarnate and the Lamb of God who takes away the sin of the world."[5] I agree with Miroslav Volf in this regard, and though, as he says, "Christ has not come with a blueprint for political arrangements,"[6] it is impossible to deny that the incarnation is the movement of God into the political realm, a movement from immateriality to materiality, heaven to earth, ephemerality to embodiment. There is no Word of God if it never touches the earth, our world, that is, politics. The incarnation reveals the necessity of the Word to be enfleshed in the political affairs of society. The incarnation shows us that even God is political.

GOSPEL AS JESUS'S POLITICAL ACT

Rooted in this understanding of the incarnation of God in Christ, one can say that not only is Jesus as the Word of God political but the gospel he preaches in word and deed is a political act as well. Who he is and what he does—the gospel—touches the earth, and even more than that, transforms

5. Volf, *Public Faith*, xv.
6. Volf, *Public Faith*, xvi.

what is on the earth and occurring in politics and our social lives together. The "gospel" or "good news" is of Jesus Christ (Mark 1:1). Jesus as the enfleshment of the gospel in word and deed is vital for understanding political engagement through a Christian lens. As Willie Jennings notes, the bodily existence of Jesus defies "walled arenas—religious, political, economic, gendered, etc."[7] Just as the body of Jesus cannot be parceled out, the gospel is nonbifurcated as well; it is one and whole, encompassing the whole of life, including the political realm.

In the Gospel of Mark, "Jesus came to Galilee, proclaiming the good news of God, and saying, 'The time is fulfilled, and the kingdom of God has come near; repent, and believe in the good news'" (Mark 1:14–15). Jesus came preaching the gospel and he presents it as his embodiment, that is, the kingdom of God is near in him, and his words, the good news. Scholars teach how the work and person of Jesus Christ were in opposition to the political powers of the day.[8] In his coming, a new kingdom was at play and the other kingdoms were definitely threatened and disgruntled. Jesus came, not rubber-stamping the status quo oppression, but with the aim to stamp oppression out once and for all. To make it even worse, Jesus was not the type of messiah the masses expected. He was a marginal figure on the borderlands of human existence. This gospel, his gospel, the word of God, came through him, an unexpected messiah. Even the beginning of Luke 3 reveals how this word of God enters the political world in the mode of critique: "In the fifteenth year of the reign of Emperor Tiberius, when Pontius Pilate was governor of Judea, and Herod was ruler of Galilee, and his brother Philip ruler of the region of Ituraea and Trachonitis, and Lysanias ruler of Abilene, during the high priesthood of Annas and Caiaphas, the word of God came to John son of Zechariah in the wilderness" (Luke 3:1–2). This word of God did not go to the powerful and prestigious and privileged of the day. But it came to a weirdo in the wilderness, John the Baptist. The arrival of this word—to whom it went and where—was already an indictment of the political status quo and earthly lords of that time. This gospel word made a political statement by the very nature of its destination.

The gospel of Jesus Christ in word and deed is a political act just like how God "precedes us, into our urban streets, suburban playgrounds, and coastal flood plains."[9] God is at work in the world, the polis, whether we like

7. Jennings, "Speaking Gospel in the Public Arena," 189.

8. See Blount, *Go Preach!* and Myers, *Binding the Strong Man.*

9. Brown, "Discerning the Public Presence of God," 37.

it or not. Also, the politics of Jesus may not be our own. Nonetheless, his politics, his gospel tone and message, are distinct and clarifying.[10] His gospel does not shy away from public engagement with the world; his focus in ministry was right at the heart of a broken society and world. In what may be called his inaugural sermon, Jesus makes it plain. "The Spirit of the Lord is upon me, because he has anointed me to bring good news to the poor. He has sent me to proclaim release to the captives and recovery of sight to the blind, to let the oppressed go free, to proclaim the year of the Lord's favor" (Luke 4:18–19). Jesus makes it clear that his gospel touches the polis, the earth, the material realm, and all of this is connected to the spiritual life in God. In particular, Jesus's politics are aligned with the marginalized—the poor, the captives, the blind, and the oppressed. The focus of his ministry is on those who have been downtrodden by the politically powerful and privileged. He spoke this political gospel and he was this political gospel. None of this should be surprising in that Jesus was a poor, oppressed Jew, a member of the disinherited class. Like him, his gospel was centered on the weak and those "with their backs against the wall."[11] Jesus was political through his articulation and embodiment of the gospel of God. Ever since his time and in his Spirit, preaching the gospel of Jesus has therefore been political.

PREACHING AS A POLITICAL ACT

With this essay's operative understanding of the political in mind, in conjunction with the incarnation as God's political act and the gospel as Jesus's political act, the ministerial practice of Christian preaching is fundamentally political at its heart since it is grounded in Jesus. To be political does not mean to politicize. By the latter, I mean an explicit emphasis on particular political parties and politicians. The danger in this politicizing approach is that the gospel can be collapsed into a political party and is then distorted by being equated with Republican or Democrat when the gospel is neither. Jesus is neither Republican nor Democrat, nor liberal nor conservative, nor a politician, but he is political in that he reveals his bias for the weak and dispossessed and this preference makes the powerful angry. He is clearly on the side of the oppressed and not the oppressor, and this is inherently a political gesture in the public realm. Jesus demonstrates another way of

10. See Hendricks, *Politics of Jesus.*

11. Thurman, *Jesus and the Disinherited*, 11.

being in the world, another kingdom, thus the "kings" of this world are threatened because they know another King is in town, which is why Herod wants to kill Jesus (Matt 2:1–15). Jesus is not afraid to engage the polis, the public square, and likewise his life is a challenging call for our preaching of the gospel to do the same. Moreover, the very practice of preaching is a political gesture because it is a nonviolent practice.[12] Through preaching, one struggles with the powers that be through words, not guns or weapons of mass destruction.

Preaching as a political act is a delicate verbal dance in the pulpit. It is so tempting to drop bombs of linguistic terrorism against political leaders with whom we vehemently disagree, and to demonize other human beings, regardless of who they are. With this approach, preaching becomes politicized, especially if leaders are targets of name-calling, which is sometimes doing the same thing as the ones we hate have done. The danger in politicizing the pulpit in this manner is that we become the very thing we hate and hearers may interpret our sermons as political stump speeches veering away from the gospel. This is by no means to mute the fact that all preaching is political, having to deal with our world, but when one dehumanizes the dehumanizer or oppresses the oppressor, then what occurs is not the gospel, even if one receives praise for doing so.

Preachers of the gospel are called to proclaim against the principalities and powers at work in our world, and not necessarily people. There are theologians and practitioners that will disagree with me on this, but it is critical to acknowledge the larger context for preaching—that is, the principalities and powers. As Ephesians reminds us, "For our struggle is not against enemies of blood and flesh, but against the rulers, against the authorities, against the cosmic powers of this present darkness, against the spiritual forces of evil in the heavenly places" (6:12). Of course, the powers will use people as pawns to oppress and depress; however, preaching as a political act recognizes that human faces will change, presidents will change, rulers will change, but the same evil can still remain, fueling the unjust systems and structures at work in the world.

For example, removing Confederate monuments from public view is merely a cosmetic act and does not change structural inequities and injustice. If one believes that removing monuments solves the racial "problem of the color line"[13] this is naïve because oppressive powers are still at work

12. Campbell, *Word Before the Powers.*
13. Dubois, *Souls of Black Folks,* xi.

in institutions, such as the prison system. This is why maintaining a focus on the powers that oppress is key when thinking about how and what to preach. Preaching is political and the call to preach politically is a call to proclaim against the powers; it is a political revolutionary practice of resistance. Framing preaching as a political act in this way shapes a practice that is loving, ultimately, and does not seek to harm the harmers, especially if our end goal is love. Thus, it's critical to keep in mind that our means of preaching should match our end of preaching.

None of this is to say that people will not get angry or upset at political preaching, even in the way I describe it in this essay. Just as people praised Jesus, the same people also raged against him (Luke 4:15, 28). It is par for the homiletical course, the course of the old-rugged cross. Mixed responses are inevitable. People will get angry, frustrated, leave the church, call you names, and threaten to stop giving money to the church. This should not be a shock as the gospel is sharper than a two-edged sword (Heb 4:12 KJV). It cuts and soothes, challenges and comforts. It is prophetic and priestly. Jesus, the enfleshed Word, gets in trouble with religious and civic powers because his word touches and troubles the status quo of the day. There will be cheers and jeers for any sermon offered and one that engages the polis may stir even more responses! What is required, therefore, is the virtue of courage. David Buttrick, in *Preaching the New and the Now*, writes that "social courage" is needed to proclaim the kingdom of God's social, political vision.[14] God's sociopolitical vision is reflected in Matt 25, " . . . 'I was hungry and you gave me food, I was thirsty and you gave me something to drink, I was a stranger and you welcomed me, I was naked and you gave me clothing, I was sick and you took care of me, I was in prison and you visited me.' . . . 'Truly I tell you, just as you did it to one of the least of these who are members of my family, you did it to me'" (25:35–40). These are material, social, political realities in the world and these are to be dealt with in our preaching.

One example of courageous preaching as a political act is shared when Howard Thurman retells how his grandmother, a former slave, heard slave preachers and was emboldened by them. The enslaved preacher would proclaim the story of Calvary to the enslaved. "But this preacher, when he had finished, would pause, his eyes scrutinizing every face in the congregation, and then he would tell them, 'You are not niggers! You are not slaves! You

---

14. Buttrick, *Preaching the New and the Now,* ix.

are God's children!'"[15] This message during slavery reveals how preaching speaks to the political or the public square and it does so to affirm the human dignity of the marginalized of the day. It resisted the oppressive powers and messages of the white master-preachers but affirmed and humanized the enslaved. This took great "social courage" and was a risky act of life and death. Preachers proclaimed the gospel while resisting other denigrating messages that were being preached.

There is not total agreement on how to approach preaching and politics within the church, as I have already mentioned, yet Dr. King makes a key argument for political engagement and he does so on the margins of a newspaper while in a Birmingham jail. Truth rings out of prison. In this letter, King wrote to white clergymen about his perspective on the gospel and its relationship to the political realm and what needed to happen next in the struggle for civil rights. He refused to "wait," as many were saying, because "wait" often meant "never" and he challenged the white religious moderates who appeared to be more "devoted to order than justice" and critiqued their "lukewarm acceptance" of the unjust social realities of their day.[16] King's sermon on paper continues preaching throughout history from the fingertips of a modern-day prophet who understood the costs for preaching the political gospel in public. He understood that preaching was risky just as it was for Jesus, but he also knew that it was worth taking the gospel public. It was worth life, even for the life of the world, the polis.

A CONCLUDING WORD: PREACHING IN PUBLIC

Speaking of preaching as a political act is rooted in a God who went public with incarnate love in Jesus Christ to reveal another realm, theological and political. God knew that if the enfleshed gospel was worth something, it could not be a private venture alone. It had to go public because it was for the world. The very nature of being political implies being public. This does not mean preaching has to occur on city street corners or in sports stadiums, but it does mean that preaching has to be out in the open for all ears to hear and eyes to see. Preaching is not a private affair. It is a public act before people. It is a word that is a Word only when it is enfleshed, when it is seen and heard in the world. Otherwise, it is not the gospel word.

15. Thurman, *With Head and Heart*, 21.

16. King, "Letter from a Birmingham Jail."

This public context also means it includes public content, having to do with social, political, and material real-world issues. John Bowlin writes,

> the church is justified in making the people's business its own, that it is authorized to do so, precisely because the Word of God that it proclaims has jurisdiction over all the world and because the people in the pew who hear that Word have hyphenated identities. They are not only Christians but also citizens, and they bring the public's business with them as they make their way through the front doors, down the aisles, and into the pews. There is no keeping the public out of the church; its walls are as porous as the souls within.[17]

This is not a surprise as preaching the gospel involves preaching at the intersection of the biblical text and the context of the world. It is the wedding of text and context, a homiletical antiphonal relationship between the biblical world and our world. A preacher is a "public imaginer"[18] for the church, which is a public entity in and of itself. Even further, Willie Jennings sees the convergence of the form of the gospel and the form of a slave in Jesus Christ as significant for "speaking gospel in the public arena." He writes,

> There is a sense in which all preaching is public address, aimed at any would-be listeners whether in ecclesial settings or nonreligious spaces. But public address rooted in the slave's position aims at a much more intense public reality—that of addressing the powers that enslave people economically, politically, socially, spiritually, and physically. This kind of public address by its very nature exposes networks of oppression and violence that run through any given society and connects people through the gospel to a shared work of announcing the will of God for human flourishing.[19]

Preaching in public is an acknowledgment that the people of God are drawn forward "into public space—out of its meaning enclaves, re-enchanted liturgies, or gated communities of resident aliens."[20] A worshiping community may gather, hear the word proclaimed, respond to that word, but then are sent into the world to scatter good news lavishly all over it. Preaching in the pulpit is a beginning that leads to proclamation of the

17. Bowlin, "Proclaiming the Gospel, Preaching the Public," 12.
18. Davis, "Preacher as Public Imaginer."
19. Jennings, "Speaking Gospel in the Public Arena," 189.
20. Jacobsen, "Going Public with the Means of Grace," 381.

gospel in the world by living it out in word and deed. It is a reminder that there is always the "go" principle in the life of faith, including preaching. Jesus may say "come" sometimes (Matt 11:28), but he often says, "Go" (Mark 16:15). Preaching must "go," go beyond the narrow confines of privatism and into all the world, the highways and byways of life, following the God enfleshed in Jesus Christ, who did the same in love. God loved the world, so God got political. So, is preaching political? Yes!

AN AFTERWORD: A POLITICAL SERMON

(This sermon was preached at the Festival of Homiletics in Washington, DC, on May 25, 2018)

"Pledging Allegiance" (Matthew 22:15–22)

The gospel lesson for today presents some topics that we are told should never be discussed in public, or at least with extended family members during the holidays—money, politics, and religion. But it's unavoidable. Jesus has a way of confronting us at our core. We can run but we can't hide this morning in our Festival of Homiletics wooden pew. Jesus doesn't shy away from controversy or crises; but he often comes with calm in the midst of challenging storms. Even while under the controlling gaze of Roman imperialism, he's not afraid; not afraid to speak the truth and nothing but the truth. That shouldn't be surprising because he is the truth. And when the truth speaks in Washington, DC, we better listen.

"Give therefore to the emperor the things that are the emperor's, and to God the things that are God's." Or in God's language, the King James Version, "Render therefore unto Caesar the things which are Caesar's; and unto God the things that are God's." On the surface, it would appear that the emperor and God are on equal footing; that is, that in some way they have the same priority. Give to the emperor his things and give to God what is God's. Plain and simple, isn't it? Not really.

The coin brought to Jesus is a silver Roman *denarius* depicting the emperor's image (his head) and bearing the inscription "Tiberius Caesar, Son of the Deified Augustus, [who also is] Augustus." On the reverse side of the coin, it declares Tiberius is "high priest," making the assertion that the emperor is divinity, is Lord, is the holy mediator of the Roman state religion. As you can imagine, this coin was blasphemous from the view of Jewish monotheism; many Jews rejected and resented it. But a rejection of the coin, the mighty dollar, was viewed as a rejection of the emperor and the Roman Empire overall. To use the coin was an act of economic enthronement of Caesar, the emperor, as Lord. Thus, economy was linked to religiosity and the perpetuation of imperial civic religion.

Those of you who are Baptists might be familiar with what is called "the love offering," an offering collected in congregations for guest preachers. When the offering is collected and the offering plates are passed, if there isn't enough love shown at the end of the collection, the offering plates are sent around again! "Love" is used to grow the economy! Believe me—there's a link in the church between economy and religious practice. Just read the book of my Duke colleague, Kate Bowler, called *Blessed: The History of the American Prosperity Gospel.*

Money, politics, and religion are interweaved and were interwoven in the ancient Roman imperial web, and a refusal to bow to this empire caused lots of problems. For early Christians, if Jesus Christ was Lord, this meant that Caesar could not be. Caesar was creature, not Creator; and one cannot serve two masters. What Jesus says reveals the ongoing struggle between competing loyalties. In other words, to whom or what do you pledge allegiance? Is it the state, the empire, the emperor, your boss, your coach, your parents, your bishop, your identity? Or is it God, is it Jesus Christ? Some may not have sold themselves to the devil, but they have sold themselves to the empire, and by doing so have enthroned the emperor, presidents, prime ministers, and other world leaders in the glow of civic glory, which is its own form of worship. Some bow at the altars of culture or country and subsume and sacrifice the Christ on these, blurring the lines so much so that it's hard to know who or what we are honoring. Confusion comes when one equates the empire-state, the nation, with the kingdom of God. It's like saying the United States of America is the kingdom of heaven; and if this is heaven, I sure don't want to know what hell is like. This country and Christ are not the same and Jesus makes it clear that the emperor, that Caesar, is different from God, thus the emperor is not the Lord.

My twelve-year-old son has been playing little league baseball in Durham, North Carolina, for the last four years or so. And you know you are in the South when at the start of each game, the players say a pledge that begins with, "I trust in God, I love my country . . . " The inculcation of religious and civic confusion starts at a very young age and can lead young people to think that God and country are the same thing. But I'm here to tell the truth this morning—they are not the same!

This may be a bit hard to digest when we rely on the country, the nation, or empire for comfort and security and protection and pleasure and even hope for a better future. It can be hard when we, even unknowingly, turn an empire into a god.

"Give therefore to the emperor the things that are the emperor's, and to God the things that are God's." "The things that are God's." Well, everything is God's, even what is the emperor's, and even the emperor! It all belongs to God. We all belong to God. God overshadows the rights and allegiances any empire might demand for itself. God determines what is Caesar's and what is not. God is sovereign over the state.

Jesus asks, when presented the coin, "Whose head is this, and whose title?" The head of the emperor can be captured on a coin held in human hands, whereas we sing, "God's got the whole world in his hands." This earthly Roman lord can be contained on a piece of metal, a coin, whereas the heavenly Lord, Jesus Christ, cannot be contained even by the highest heaven (2 Chr 6:18). There is no graven image of God that can encapsulate the totality of God and we definitely can't hold God in our feeble hands. Rather, God holds us, his precious jewels made in his image.

Beginning with the early church father Tertullian, many have identified "the things that are God's" with human beings. If coins with Caesar's image and inscription belong to Caesar, then human beings created in God's image, as we see in Genesis, belong entirely to God. Give to God the things that are God's. In other words, give yourself to God for we are God's, and Jesus calls his hearers to a higher fidelity, transcending adherence to any imperial law or figure. He calls us to look beyond an image on any coin to whose image is on every human being. We can get lost in a market-driven life and political power plays and align ourselves to the empire, and forget in whose image we have been created. When we do that, we give ourselves over to the emperor rather than God. But if we remember God's words, "Let us make humankind in our image, according to our likeness," (Gen 1:26) we will remember that we belong to God and should offer ourselves to God. Our deepest self is God's for the imprint of God's image is on us. As one seminary professor writes, "We may divide our budget, but we must never divide our allegiance."[21]

21. Pape, "Commentary on Matthew 22:15–22," para. 12.

How can we pledge allegiance to the empire and to God? And why would we do that anyway? Notice that it's the Pharisees, their disciples, and the Herodians (think King Herod's groupies), who try to entrap Jesus. The religious and civic authorities collude against Jesus. When Jesus points us to the things that are God's, he moves our theological and social imagination to a higher plane to remind us that state and religious leaders can be agents of injustice and even evil. He gestures beyond humanity and human leadership or governance because institutional religious bodies, the church, and government do not necessarily always remind us that we belong to God, because they want us to belong to them—our time, our energy, our gifts, our taxes, our everything. But you don't belong to your denomination and you don't belong to your bishop and you don't belong to your synod and you don't belong to your congregation. You belong to God!

What Jesus knew and what Jesus knows is that allegiance to God will also sometimes mean resistance to civic and religious authorities because the earthly empire is not the heavenly kingdom of God. Sometimes following Jesus means you might have to resist the church which has lost its way. During the Civil Rights movement of the 1960s, the Rev. Dr. Martin Luther King Jr. was imprisoned, and in his "Letter from the Birmingham Jail," he writes, "So often the contemporary church is a weak, ineffectual voice with an uncertain sound. So often it is an arch defender of the status quo. Far from being disturbed by the presence of the church, the power structure of the average community is consoled by the church's silent—and often even vocal—sanction of things as they are."[22]

Dr. King reveals that following Jesus isn't necessarily the same thing as following the church. I say this because the Pharisees and their disciples—the religious folk, the church deacon board—along with the empire-state, the Herodians, are both complicit in putting Jesus to death. They not only test Jesus but eventually torture him. In the end, the religious and civic bodies conspire against Jesus as he obeys the will of God. There is socio-political and religious wrath against Jesus; Jesus knows this is the reality of the empire that has subsumed politics *and* religion under its powerful oppressive regime and he learns a lesson from *Star Wars*—that the empire will strike back.

The movie *Romero* is based on the true story of the Catholic Archbishop Oscar Romero of El Salvador, who resisted the civic, religious, and military powers that oppressed and tortured the poor. At one point, Romero is

22. King, "Letter from a Birmingham Jail," para. 32.

put in prison along with one of his colleagues. As he stands in his prison cell, exhausted, drenched in sweat and despair, he begins to hear his friend scream with terror as he's tortured by his captors. In that moment, Romero yells out from his cell, "We're human beings! We're human beings!"[23] The empire doesn't see us as human beings but as commodities, tools for production, not as people made in the image of God. And this becomes even clearer when in 1980, Archbishop Romero is assassinated while presiding at the Eucharist. The empire will strike back and this shouldn't surprise us.

Emperors and the empire don't save, have never saved, will never save, and in the end, if you bow to it, if you give yourself to it, it will still eventually kill you, just like it did Jesus. So, let's put an end to the fake news that declares the emperor is God, and that the empire-state, the nation, and the kingdom of God are synonymous. Let's put an end to the fake news that equates patriotism and love of country with being a Christian and loving God, even though being an American is not the same thing as being a Christian. Let's put an end to the fake news that says worship of the American flag is the same thing as the worship of God. Let's put an end to the fake news that certain physical symbols, though historical, powerful and meaningful, are more important than real human lives today.

And let's start spreading the faith news. The faith news that there is one gospel, one Lord, one Savior, and it's not Caesar, and it's not Rome, it's not any one country or nation, but it is the Lord Jesus Christ. Countries and states will let you down. Churches and denominations will let you down, but they are not the Lord. Jesus is.

So, I pledge allegiance to him today. I take a knee at the altar of eternity around the table for the marriage supper of the Lamb. I don't need any coins to buy food or drink because Jesus gives himself to us. His body will feed us. His blood will quench our thirst. I pledge allegiance today. I bow in reverence and in praise to the Lamb of God who was slain.

> I pledge allegiance to the Lamb
> With all my strength, with all I am
> I will seek to honor His commands
> I pledge allegiance to the Lamb.[24]

---

23. Diugan, *Romero*, .
24. Ray Boltz, "I Pledge Allegiance to the Lamb," Warner/Chappell Music, Inc., 1994.

4

Postmodern Wisdom Homiletics

O. WESLEY ALLEN JR.

SINGLEHANDEDLY, ALYCE M. MCKENZIE has gotten preachers and homileticians to attend to the wisdom literature of the Bible when most trends move in other directions. While she has other areas of homiletical expertise, especially in the arena of creativity in preaching,[1] the focus on wisdom literature has extended from her first book, *Preaching Proverbs: Wisdom for the Pulpit*, to one of her most recent ones, *Wise Up! Four Biblical Virtues for Navigating Life*.

In this essay, I want to deal with an understated yet recurring element of McKenzie's scholarship on a homiletical approach related to wisdom— the potential relationship between wisdom literature and the preacher as sage on the one hand, and postmodernism on the other. I will begin with an exploration of cultural postmodernism; examine Proverbs, Job, and Ecclesiastes for ways postmodernism would find affinity with them, primarily using McKenzie's description of these works; and, finally, examine three different postmodern homiletics through the lens of these three pieces of wisdom literature.

---

1. See McKenzie, *Novel Preaching* and McKenzie, *Making a Scene in the Pulpit*.

CULTURAL POSTMODERNISM

According to Ernest Gellner, "Postmodernism is a contemporary movement. It is strong and fashionable. Over and above this, it is not altogether
clear what the devil it is."[2] Gellner has a point: scholars disagree about
which elements of postmodern worldviews are most constitutive, and postmodernism is in its infancy and still has much maturation to undergo. Still,
I think it is both possible and helpful to develop a broad, working sketch
of postmodernism as a cultural or folk epistemology active in twenty-first-
century Western cultures (as opposed to detailing various scholarly arguments for and about postmodernity).[3] One way to start this sketch is to
take the "post" element of the term seriously and remind ourselves what
*post*modernism moves past (although it is difficult in this infancy stage to
know to what degree the "post" will mean a rejection or revision of what
came before). The name makes explicit that postmodernism moves past
modernism, but implicit is the fact that is also continues modernism's move
past premodernism.

Premodernism, the dominant worldview of the pre-Enlightenment
and prescientific eras (but with elements persisting in various pockets of
society, such as fundamentalism, still today), is an epistemology in which
truth is viewed as absolute. Whatever is true in Jerusalem must, by definition, be true in Athens, Babylon, Cairo, Persia, Antioch, and Rome. While
observation and experience certainly played a role in determining what is
true, the final determinant of truth in this worldview is revelation. "God
said it. I believe it. And that settles it."

There were/are obviously contradictory claims about what has been
divinely revealed in different faith traditions and even within a single faith
tradition. On the one hand, to premoderns this simply means that someone
is right and someone is wrong. On the other hand, premoderns also rec-
ognized human finitude and saw heaven and earth as filled with mystery.
Both heaven and earth had power over their lives they could not fully understand, so naturally some assertions will be wrong. This combination of

2. I referenced this quote at the beginning of my first work dealing with postmodernism—*Homiletic of All Believers*, 3—based on its use by McKenzie in a paper she delivered
at the Academy of Homiletics in 2004, which was subsequently published as "'Different
Strokes for Different Folks,'" 201.

3. In other words, I am interested in what Paul Lakeland refers to as "cultural postmodernism" in *Postmodernity*, and what Ronald J. Allen calls "folk postmodernism" in
Allen et al., *Theology for Preaching*.

confidence in absolute truth and the recognition of mystery often made for an odd dynamic of apologetics and syncretism in the ancient world.

Like premodernism, modernist epistemology holds to a view of truth as absolute. Whatever is true on Earth must also be true on Mars, Jupiter, Pluto, and the farthest point in the universe. In modernity, however, truth is determined by reason instead of divine revelation. Empirical observation, the scientific method, and mathematics join forces to influence every field of study, faith community, and the ways individuals engage the world. For example, humanities, including biblical studies, strived to be "scientific" and objective in their endeavors. Preachers and theologians reinterpreted classic texts of different faiths in light of new scientific discoveries (i.e., reason forces reconsideration of what had been considered divinely revealed).

Great confidence in the human mind, and consequently in human ability, characterizes modernism. If we can know the world through our own means we can control the world by our own means. Mystery as an explanation for what we do not know is replaced with the idea that science has yet to discover everything. The heavens and earth do not have power over us; we have power over them. Nowhere is this power more evident than in the technological advances of modernity that extend from the printing press to farming techniques, industrialized production means, conquering the skies with flight, and mass media. Significant humanistic hope in our ability to defeat hunger, poverty, and the like accompanied this epistemology.

The confidence in our ability to conquer the world, however, did not diminish human desire to conquer other humans. Advanced technology did not lead to every belly being full and every back clothed. While certainly some advances were made in this type of work, more energy and resources were put in advancing the technology of warfare than advancing the welfare of the entire human population. With the twentieth century's two world wars, mass genocides, nuclear armament, and Cold War, confidence in human reason to fix all our ills was destroyed. Along with it, any remaining sense of a God in control of everything that happens was destroyed for many people trying to hold on to a premodern sense of mystery and revelation. The combination of intense views of human evil and sustained theodicy (along with other various strains of globalization) has, likewise, led to a challenging rejection of the underpinnings of modernism for many people, whether conscious or not.

What has been slowly evolving since the early twentieth century, and developing more quickly for the last forty to fifty years, has been called "postmodernism." This epistemology has evolved far enough that some are willing to speak of our current age and culture as "postmodernity," although premodern and modern claims are still spoken in the public square loudly and with force.

While still evolving, postmodernism may well mark a more dramatic epistemological shift from modernism and premodernism than was modernism's shift from premodernism. Whereas the earlier shift represented a transition in the way we approach truth, the current shift is in many ways a transition away from truth itself, at least as truth has been understood for thousands of years. A college student of mine who was a biology major and called herself a fundamentalist was debating evolution in a religion and science class. When a student pressed her on how she could be a biologist and still believe God created the world in six days, she replied, "Evolution may be true for you but it is not true for me." That we have reached a point where a fundamentalist—even a young, naïve fundamentalist—could use such language shows the significance of the shift underway.

The student's language illustrates what many describe as the epistemological understanding of truth as relative, local, and/or subjective. Truth is no longer absolutely true everywhere and for all times, but is true for me/us here and now. I would argue, however, that while many are still using the word "truth," the shift of emphasis is really from absolute truth to personal, socially constructed *meaningfulness*. Citizens of postmodernity care less about what is true, correct, or right, and care more about what makes sense and what works for me at this moment, in this place. Objectivity searching for truth is a myth replaced with contextualized functionality.

Postmoderns, therefore, are less concerned with rational, logical consistency and more with making ever-evolving meaning of their experience. Revelation and reason intended for all as the authority for determining what is true is replaced with my or our (my particular identity group's) experience determining what is meaningful for me/us. There is little desire to be instructed by others in, or to proffer to others, a metanarrative that, like a grand theory in physics, provides the basis of a worldview for all. I choose my own metanarrative through which to view the world or choose to have no metanarrative at all and am glad to give others the same freedom. This is why postmoderns feel free to draw together into a worldview elements from what modernists would have considered opposing and irreconcilable metanarratives. It is a smorgasbord approach to assembling a worldview. Indeed, there is great suspicion of top-down approaches that try to prescribe truth for others—authority is a bad word to postmoderns.

This move past modernism can lead to significant pessimism. With confidence in objective human reason diminished or lost, so is confidence in human ability to fix the world's problems. A focus on relative meaning (i.e., meaning related to me/us) sees global issues as beyond the scope of my concern or unfixable on the basis of its size when contrasted with the size of my/our individually constructed meaning and sense of abilities.

Having developed a sketch of what we might consider to be some identifying markers of postmodernism, we should nuance our working definition a bit by noting that people embrace postmodern epistemologies to varying degrees. Many, if not most, people in North America have one foot in the pond of modernism while the other is in the river of postmodernism. Different people put more weight on one foot than the other. Some are wading with both feet into postmodernism, while still others have jumped in completely and are covered in it head to toe. Thus identifying a "typical" postmodern is at best a helpful heuristic device.

POSTMODERNISM AND WISDOM LITERATURE

It is common, for instance, for wisdom scholars to note that wisdom literature does not appeal to the covenantal theology or salvation history schema related to the exodus, the metanarrative that undergirds so much of the Hebrew Bible narrative, prophetic, and poetic works. Rooting theology in something other than such metanarratives has appeal to postmodern thinkers.

McKenzie differentiates between emphases in the three major wisdom works in the Hebrew Bible.[4] Proverbs is the most traditional form of wisdom that grows out of a community of sages. Ecclesiastes is representative of the wisdom tradition of having a cool (i.e., disciplined and dispassionate) spirit. And Job (and to some degree Ecclesiastes) represents the subversive voice(s) in the wisdom tradition. Job's approach to suffering, for example, subverts readers' views of God as "consistent and righteous." Similarly Leon Roper and Alphonso Groenewald draw a bold line between Proverbs as traditional wisdom on the one hand and Job and Ecclesiastes as

---

4. The following is distilled from McKenzie, *Hear and Be Wise.*

"wisdom in revolt" on the other.[5] In this revolt, they argue, Job and Ecclesiastes especially have similarities with postmodern thought.[6] Building on these different insights, I want to propose a schema in which three different strands in cultural postmodernism have affinities to the three biblical wisdom writings.

Proverbs. As the oldest collection of wisdom materials and therefore most traditional form of wisdom in the collection under consideration, the book of Proverbs likely represents the work of sages across numerous generations that attained its final form in the postexilic community. The origin of individual proverbs is impossible to determine, but it is clear that Israelite sages and scribes were influenced by older wisdom traditions in other Near Eastern cultures (e.g., Mesopotamia, Egypt, and Canaan), so much so that this tradition of thought could predate the Torah traditions.[7]

Instead of being based on God's revelatory action in history (as is Torah), the sages' wisdom collected in Proverbs drew on common cultural stock, offering human reflections of human experience in attempts to deal with questions of ethics, how to cope with life, and how to be successful. These reflections are not offered as universal dictums. They likely originate out of specific occasions of observation but are assumed to have broader potential usefulness. As McKenzie states, "Proverbs are partial generalizations, not universal truths for all situations. The proverb's usefulness in new situations is referred to as its 'openness to experience,' or its '*hermeneutical openness.*'"[8] So a proverb is useful in a range of situations until it is not. This dynamic allows for wisdom at times to be contradictory (e.g., Prov 26:4 placed right next to 26:5).

The fact that Proverbs draws so clearly from and focuses so on human experience has led some to see it at odds with the revelatory tradition in the Hebrew Bible.[9] This, however, is an overstatement rooted in an argument from silence. The absence in Proverbs of discourse dealing with the

5. Roper and Groenewald, "Job and Ecclesiastes as (Postmodern?) Wisdom in Revolt."

6. Roper and Groenewald, "Job and Ecclesiastes as (Postmodern?) Wisdom in Revolt," 5–8.

7. Per a personal conversation with Roy L. Heller on November 28, 2018; see also Clifford, "Introduction to Wisdom Literature," 3–7.

8. McKenzie, *Preaching Proverbs*, 5.

9. For example, Norman K. Gottwald claims this wisdom tradition runs against the grain of other religious domains in Israel to the point of being "nonrevelatory" (*Hebrew Bible*, 566).

covenantal/salvific strands of theology of the Hebrew tradition could as easily mean the sages and redactors assumed it as resisted it. Or it could mean, as implied above when discussing the dating of the wisdom tradition, that the sages pulling together different strands of wisdom thought were simply unaware of the exodus tradition and such. Either way, we need not assume tension between Israel's revelatory tradition and Proverbs, so much as recognizing that historical revelation is not mentioned in Proverbs. There are, however, two theological elements in the book that temper any assertion that the collection of proverbs claims a fully human origin with no connection to divine revelation. First, the role of Woman Wisdom in Prov 1–9 and 31 implies wisdom is a gift to humanity from God. Second, Proverbs has a high theology of creation, if you will.[10] Subtly threaded through the collection is a view that God has established a world order, including an ordering of right and wrong, righteousness and evil. The proverbs attempt to order human life (or some element of it) in accordance with this divinely ordained order.[11] In fact, many of the proverbs seem to assume the order of the world can be translated into a clear cause-and-effect approach to behavior: do this action and that end will be achieved (as set up by the Creator).

Those postmoderns who keep one foot firmly rooted in modernism might well be attracted to this form of wisdom. A metanarrative could still be assumed without being strongly asserted. In its place, theology drawn from human experience takes the foreground. These experiences can be gathered from a smorgasbord of sources, might be contradictory at times, and are weighed by usefulness.

Job. The book of Job shares many of the qualities of traditional wisdom found in Proverbs. There is no discussion of YHWH's history of saving the Israelites or making covenant with them (even in relation to Job's suffering). Instead, the theologizing that occurs is rooted in human reflection on human experience.

The primary views associated with traditional wisdom, however, are represented by Job's conversation partners, with whom Job argues (chs. 3–37). They interpret Job's suffering through the lens of cause and effect, righteousness vs. evil, reward and punishment. Job must have done something, they assume and assert, or YHWH would not have punished him.

Job (both the character and the book) does not reject this wisdom-rooted theology but claims YHWH has been wrong in judging him. The

---

10. See Perdue, *Wisdom and Creation.*
11. Murphy, "Wisdom Theses," 187–200.

quite impatient Job makes clear to his "comforters" that he has done nothing to deserve his plight even though they refuse to accept a world in which
such suffering would be coincidental or caused by God in a manner inconsistent with one's actions. The narrative prologue to the book (chs. 1–2),
however, makes clear that Job is correct: his suffering is not punishment
for sin.[12]

At stake, then, is the very question of the character of God. Job deals
with the problem of reconciling a loving, just God with the suffering of
the righteous. YHWH is actually the character in the story who challenges
wisdom theology most directly. In the dialogue with Job in chapters 38–42,
YHWH describes the divine character in terms of creation. In this sense the
theology of the book of Job fits with the underlying emphasis on creation
we saw in Proverbs. The difference is that in Job, YHWH does not present a created order that justifies wisdom's view of cause and effect when it
comes to suffering as punishment. Instead YHWH claims that creation and
YHWH's role in creating and presiding over the world are too complex for
Job to understand, too complex to be reduced to simple wisdom formulas.
And thus the phenomena of suffering and success cannot be reduced to
easy punishment and reward theologies.

Those postmoderns who have most of their weight on the foot in postmodernism but still keep the big toe of their other foot dipped in the waters
of modernism might well be attracted to this form of wisdom. Theology
drawn from experience is primary but without completely abandoning any
sense of all universals (God is still Creator). Still, such a sense of universals
(metanarrative) is approached with a hermeneutic of suspicion. It is de-
constructed (without being completely demolished) to lay bare ways it has
upheld power structures underlying theological assertions: the successful
claim righteousness and divine reward for themselves and condemn those
less fortunate as sinful and punished.

Ecclesiastes. Whereas Job is still clinging to aspects of a wisdom
worldview even as he challenges it, Qoheleth rejects it altogether. If Job is
wisdom subverted or wisdom in revolt, we might think of Ecclesiastes as
anti-wisdom.

Like Job, Ecclesiastes rejects a simplistic view of reward and punishment. The wise may suffer and the foolish prosper. But Qoheleth walks
further down that road repeatedly claiming that all is vanity (1:2, 14; 2:1,

12. While the narrative frame of the book is likely a later addition to an older poetic
document, my concern is with the final, canonical form of the book.

11, 15, 17, 19, 21, 23, 26; 3:19; 4:4, 7, 8, 16; 5:10; 6:2, 4, 9, 11; 7:6; 8:10, 14; 9:2; 11:10; 12:8). As James L. Crenshaw describes the central view of Ecclesiastes, "Life is profitless; totally absurd . . . Enjoy life as you can, advises the author, for old age will soon overtake you. And even as you enjoy, know that the world is meaningless. Virtue does not bring reward. The deity stands distant, abandoning humanity to chance and death."[13] Later Crenshaw adds, "Job attacks God directly, remaining on speaking terms with his adversary and ultimately provoking dialogue. Qoheleth refuses to address the deity, complaining instead to his own heart."[14] In Job, there is at least a remnant of the view that a divinely established connection between deed and consequence remains (even if it is mainly exerted in the narrative portions), but in Ecclesiastes this view is abandoned altogether.[15]

Ecclesiastes' disillusionment with wisdom thought does not lead to an agnostic or atheistic rejection of the idea of God. Instead, God is seen as inscrutable and distant. Unlike a deist position in which God acts in creating the world and then leaves the world to run itself, Qoheleth's God continues to act, but in ways that are inconsistent, seemingly arbitrary, and maybe even indefensible. What is certainly clear for Qoheleth is that God has not prescribed a way of life (such as found in Proverbs) that guarantees meaning and success in life. Indeed, because death cancels out everything achieved in life, life has no inherent meaning.

This view does not lead Qoheleth, however, to promote some full-blown form of libertine hedonism. McKenzie at one point summarizes the three "facts of life" that Ecclesiastes forces us to face: "1. Life is unpredictable; 2. God is unknowable; and 3) Death is inevitable." Asking what Qoheleth claims is the goal of the life well-lived is, McKenzie answers, "It comes in two parts. First we face the facts of life we would much prefer to ignore. Only then can we do part two, which is to live each present moment aware of our human limitations and the precious, if precarious, joy an inscrutable God has granted us as our portion in this unpredictable life (3:9–14)."[16]

Those postmoderns who have fully pulled both feet out of the waters of modernity and have waded into postmodernity up to their hips will be more attracted to Ecclesiastes than Proverbs or Job. Theology drawn from

13. Crenshaw, *Ecclesiastes*, 23.

14. Crenshaw, *Ecclesiastes*, 24.

15. Roper and Groenewald, "Job and Ecclesiastes as (Postmodern?) Wisdom in Revolt," 5.

16. McKenzie, *Preaching Biblical Wisdom in a Self-Help Society,* 151–53.

experience is primary, and hardly any sense of all universals remains at all (except there is nothing new under the sun; 1:9). Deconstruction of and disillusion concerning previous worldviews reigns in this work. And any meaning to life, if not given from above and discovered by us, is construct-ed by us in the face of arbitrariness of existence and the reality of death.

POSTMODERN, SAPIENTIAL HOMILETICS

As an advocate for the biblical wisdom literature, McKenzie rightfully argues that preachers should offer sermons based on texts from all three of the books discussed above. I certainly agree and think that exposing a congregation to the different views of these works can expand both their understanding of and engagement with the canon and their existential, theological reflection.

McKenzie also, however, advocates for the preacher taking on the role of sage as modeled by the biblical sages. She introduces this identity of the preacher in her early book, *Preaching Proverbs*:

> [T]he preacher as sage shapes the identity of communities of faith by cultivating an ongoing dialogue between the common wisdom of cultural groups and the biblical wisdom that informs the faith community. The preacher as sage is alert to cultural proverbs that are in common use in her congregation, both those which are compatible with and those that compete with Christian faith. Her sermons employ both kinds in shaping the community's identity over against surrounding worldviews.[17]

In *Hear and Be Wise*, McKenzie expands this view of the preacher as sage rooted in a reading of Proverbs to one based on four pillars of wisdom thought, with different pillars drawn from different wisdom writings we are considering:

First Pillar—The Bended Knee (Proverbs)

Second Pillar—The Listening Heart (Proverbs)

Third Pillar—The Cool Spirit (Ecclesiastes)

Fourth Pillar—The Subversive Voice (Job).[18]

---

17. McKenzie, *Preaching Proverbs*, xxi–xxii.

18. McKenzie, *Hear and Be Wise*.

While the book does a good job of demonstrating what preachers can learn about homiletical and didactic approaches from each of these biblical works, I am less comfortable with the move to unite them under the single heading of sage than is McKenzie. As we related the three works to different levels of postmodern commitments, so do I think the different postmodern affinities with each work suggests different sorts of postmodern homiletics, different sorts of contemporary preacher/sages.

McKenzie herself represents a homiletic rooted in a postmodern epistemology that has affinity with Proverbs. This is in part because of the way she views postmodernism itself: "Rather than a descent into the abyss of relativity, I interpret postmodernism as the recognition that theological statements arise out of concrete situations and need to be continually placed back into them for validation and correction."[19] In truth, instead of interpreting what postmodernism is, McKenzie here names the limits of what she is willing to embrace in postmodern epistemologies. She is attracted to the contextual focus of postmodernism so long as it does not become relativistic.

Similarly, in her later essay, "The Company of Sages: Homiletical Theology as a Sapiential Hermeneutic," McKenzie embraces a little of postmodern thought by arguing against viewing preaching as a hierarchical "delivery system" in which the preacher presents eternal truths to the congregation. In its place, she proposes a homiletic modeled on the biblical sages and practical theology that is contextual in orientation, acknowledges the limits of personal knowledge, and values group dialogue in making meaning. In this work she mentions Job and Ecclesiastes (as well as Jesus as sage) but draws primarily on the approach of sages represented in Proverbs. Indeed, while affirming the openness of a sapiential hermeneutic, McKenzie concludes by noting, "Our role as sages is to model biblical wisdom's version of a life well lived in keeping with God's purposes and then, through our lives and preaching, to equip our congregations to live this way too."[20]

Such language is of one who still has a foot firmly planted in modernity. McKenzie's approach to postmodern preaching (a term she would likely not apply to her work) is to revise modernist approaches to preaching by drawing on subjective, cultural experience and wisdom in ways resisted in earlier homiletical approaches, while still holding to a loyalty to an overarching metanarrative.

19. McKenzie, *Preaching Biblical Wisdom on a Self-Help Society*, 33.
20. McKenzie, "Company of Sages," 101.

My scholarship can serve as a representative of a homiletic rooted in a postmodern epistemology that has affinity with Job as I have described the work. In an early book, I propose a conversational homiletic as an appropriate approach to preaching in a postmodern age as described above.[21] I explore ways preachers can honor diverse experiences, social locations, and theologies, offering the sermon as a contribution to the ongoing matrix of conversations that is the church (and society) as opposed to making an authoritative declaration from above. While I do not use the language of wisdom in that work, my intent fits with a move to lower the authority of the preacher that rests on preaching the church's definitive metanarrative; instead, preaching is better when drawing on and hopefully contributing to the wisdom found in the community of faith and the wider culture.

In my more recent book, *Preaching and the Human Condition*, I qualify my engagement with postmodernism a bit and describe myself as a "light postmodernist":

> I am postmodern in the sense that I am less interested in debating what is true and more interested in conversing about how we construct meaning and are constructed by meaning. I am less interested in debating which metanarrative is absolute for all and more interested in offering to others a metanarrative that I have chosen as ultimate for me while listening to the metanarratives they have chosen as ultimate for them. Instead of speaking the word of God in a top-down, authoritative fashion, I am more interested in preachers viewing themselves as contributing to the matrix of conversations that comprise the congregation as a whole. Preachers have a privileged voice in these conversations in that they stand in the midst of the gathered assembly each week and contribute a monologue to the conversation, but these contributions from the pulpit are always made in the context of reciprocal listening to others in the congregation (and the world) as they also offer the word of God. All of this, however, is a light postmodernism, because I would also argue that the cornerstone upon which the church's biblical preaching is built is the assumption that our ancient texts still speak to contemporary existence because the underlying structure of human existence is persistent.[22]

The "light" part of light postmodernism allows me to propose a three-dimensional construct for homiletically exploring "the" human condition

21. Allen, *Homiletic of All Believers.*

22. Allen, *Preaching and the Human Condition,* 5.

across one's preaching ministry in terms of the broken relationship with God (vertical), broken relationships with neighbor (horizontal), and broken relationship with self (inner).

While I have a foot deeper in postmodern waters than does McKenzie, I still clearly keep a toe in the pool of modernism. My form of postmodern homiletics is a rejection of the traditional authority of the preacher whose experience is expressed monologically as paradigmatic for the passive congregation (i.e., assuming a commonality of experience) and searches for a mode in which the sermon is offered as one resource among others which individual hearers and communities of faith bring into conversation with other voices.

A representative of a homiletic rooted in a postmodern epistemology that has affinity with Ecclesiastes is Jacob D. Myers. In his book, *Preaching Must Die!: Troubling Homiletical Theology*, Myers performs a full-blown deconstruction of foundational homiletical understandings of language, identity, Scripture, and God.[23] At every point where a modernist homiletic might try to assert itself, Myers cries, "All is vanity."

Instead of attempting to build a consistent, constructive, logical argument, piece by piece, his goal is to kill off modernist preaching and homiletics in order to give life to postmodern preaching by using twists and contradictions from postmodern philosophers, offering examples from popular culture, and bringing in neglected voices from the homiletical margins. He constantly pulls the rug out from under the readers' feet, for example, by unpacking a key concept for his discussion only to qualify the concept with a parenthetical, *if there is such a thing as* _____. He also reverses his direction at times in ways that can (intentionally?) give the readers a little motion sickness, such as when in chapter 2 he argues that preaching must be viewed as an event in relation to the identity of the preacher after having argued against preaching as event when deconstructing homiletical views of language in chapter 1.

In essence Myers argues that as modernity—with its hegemony of the white, heterosexual, cisgender, economically privileged male and its myth of objectivity and epistemological foundations that serves that hegemony—must die, so must preaching and homiletics that have grown out of and contributed to that hegemony die, even to the point of forsaking any priority assigned to the oral medium of proclamation that is by definition preaching.

23. Myers, *Preaching Must Die!*

While numerous other homileticians that do scholarship and preach in the waters of postmodernism could be named, these examples serve well to show three postmodern homiletical arenas/approaches available to the church now. To borrow the language we used to described Proverbs, Job, and Ecclesiastes, those options are a traditional but sage-oriented homiletic, a homiletic in revolt, and an anti-homiletic.

5

Preaching and the Wisdom of God

A Wisdom Homiletic

EUNJOO MARY KIM

ONE OF ALYCE MCKENZIE's distinctive contributions to homiletics is her profound insight into preaching the wisdom literature in the Bible. In her masterful piece, *Hear and Be Wise*, she defines wisdom as "an expression of the presence and guidance of God" to which "human construals of wisdom are subject,"[1] and identifies the Christian preacher as "a wisdom teacher" or "a sage."[2] For McKenzie, the role of the preacher as a sage is to "empower the people of God to recognize their identities as seekers and teachers of wisdom for living" and to invite them into "the house of Wisdom,"[3] which is held up by four virtues—"the bended knee" (the fear of the Lord/humility),[4] "the listening heart" (attentiveness),[5] "the cool spirit" (self-control),[6] and

---

1. McKenzie, *Hear and Be Wise*, 11.
2. McKenzie, *Hear and Be Wise*, xiii, xv.
3. McKenzie, *Hear and Be Wise*, 14.
4. McKenzie, *Hear and Be Wise*, 17.
5. McKenzie, *Hear and Be Wise*, 61.
6. McKenzie, *Hear and Be Wise*, 107.

"the subversive voice."[7] Throughout the book, she explains these four pillars and proposes homiletical ideas in relation to each one.

McKenzie's invaluable work encourages preachers to preach from the wisdom literature in the Bible more often and in more effective ways. Moreover, her homiletical concern with wisdom challenges the church to deepen its understanding of the substance of the Christian gospel in relation to the concept of wisdom. She also encourages preachers to take seriously how to develop Christian preaching from the perspective of wisdom. The following three sections respond to theological and homiletical issues around three questions: What does wisdom mean in a theological sense? What does it mean to preach wisdom? How might wisdom be effectively communicated through preaching? I call the set of homiletical theories that can answer these questions a wisdom homiletic.

HUMAN WISDOM AND GOD'S WISDOM

What does wisdom mean in a theological sense? The word wisdom is multifaceted. People use it in different situations with a variety of meanings. While it is difficult to pin down the meaning into one fixed definition, the word "wisdom" has at least five different dimensions: 1) conventional wisdom based in human reason and experience as guidance for a better life; 2) pragmatic wisdom or skill in a specialist field obtained through practice or *techne*; 3) a moral virtue that is universally admired as "creativity, curiosity, open-mindedness, and love of learning"[8]; 4) practical wisdom or *phronesis*, which is a process of discernment for decision-making, based on the integration of knowledge, experience, and the critical understanding of a particular situation; and 5) "lived wisdom," which means "the dynamic of human knowledge, understanding and practice in relation to God and the fulfillment of God's purpose."[9]

The first four dimensions represent the anthropological view of wisdom, while the last one synthesizes this with the theological view. According to Daniel Hardy, lived wisdom is concerned with the meaning of life and a way of living responsibly for "the common good" or "the kingdom of God,"[10] and it corresponds to the theological meaning of wisdom that

7. McKenzie, *Hear and Be Wise*, 129.
8. Deane-Drummand, *Wisdom of the Liminal*, 127.
9. Hardy, "Grace of God and Earthly Wisdom," 231.
10. Hardy, "Grace of God and Earthly Wisdom," 232.

I articulate in my book, *Christian Preaching and Worship in Multicultural Contexts*. Wisdom in a theological sense is "a comprehensive and holistic perception of a way of approaching life. In other words, wisdom is concerned with a way of living or a way of assessing life in relation to who we are and what we ought to do as members of the human family."[11]

Lived wisdom is the common concern of most religions in the world. Buddhism, for example, considers lived wisdom the core of its teaching, and calls it Buddhahood. The main concern of Taoism is instruction in *Tao*, i.e., the way, path, or principle of humanity. The goal of Confucian teaching is sagehood, or the way of humanity. Hinduism and Islam seek to instruct in a way of life in the midst of the existential problems and predicaments of people's daily lives. American Indian religions give ethical guidelines for a way of life that encourages "the personal, communal, and eventually cosmic balance."[12] And the Jewish and Christian Scriptures help us understand that the term "wisdom" belongs to a way of life that emerges in many spheres of diverse human experiences.[13] The main concern of these religions is with a way of seeing reality in relation to theological and ethical questions about what it means to be human and how to live individual and communal lives responsibly as members of the human community and as an integral part of the universe.

Many Christian theologians and preachers tend to regard the divine wisdom revealed in Jesus Christ as opposed to human wisdom, or consider the latter inferior to the former. In lived wisdom, however, human and divine wisdom are inseparably bound up in a dialectical relationship. Wisdom is found in human nature when people of different race, gender, ethnicity, or socioeconomic status make the effort to discover common interests and concerns in order to fulfill the common good for humanity, by engaging in conversation with one another. Human wisdom based on practical reasoning and empathy for others seems capable of guiding the ethical life of humanity.

However, we cannot assume that this is always the case in reality. We human beings often compromise ourselves with the prevailing cultural values and accept discriminatory views without critical reflection. In such cases, as Susan Parsons points out, human wisdom is caught up in

---

11. Kim, *Christian Preaching and Worship in Multicultural Contexts*, 47.

12. Tinker, "Decolonizing the Language of Lutheran Theology," 95.

13. Bass et al., *Christian Practical Wisdom*, 8.

"projections of human pride and manipulation,"[14] and fails to guide humanity in truthful ways. The apostle Paul's critique of human wisdom in 1 Cor 1:18—2:5 illustrates a reaction to the distorted understanding and practice of human wisdom. In the cultural milieu of the Corinthian church, wisdom was understood as "the possession of exalted knowledge" and "the ability to express that knowledge in a powerful and rhetorically polished way."[15] That kind of human wisdom made those who possessed it proud and caused conflicts between the members of the church. Paul reminded them that such distorted human wisdom had nothing to do with the divine wisdom revealed in the cross of Jesus Christ.

What, then, is divine wisdom? According to Paul, it is the manifestation of the divine nature—*love*—which is fully revealed in the cross of Jesus Christ. Divine wisdom is a way of seeing through the lens of love and living it out in our daily lives. Love is not an intellectual property that can be acquired through learning, but is to be realized through practice in turning toward our neighbor in humility, generosity, and reconciliation. Divine wisdom, therefore, is in the never-ending process of practicing love in our daily lives, and its completion is an eschatological *telos*.

We humans long deeply for something that will bring life. This is only possible, according to Parsons, when human wisdom is connected to divine wisdom by means of the proclamation of "the liberating and transforming Word of God." She convinces us that the proclamation of "the complete otherness of the kingdom [of God]" reorients human nature toward the divine nature of mercy and loving-kindness and renews human wisdom as inseparable from divine wisdom.[16] Christian preaching, therefore, makes it possible to place human wisdom into the broader context of the divine intention for humanity and creation and to integrate it with the divine wisdom.

WISDOM AND PREACHING JESUS

What does it mean to preach wisdom? Some preachers might perhaps say, "Preach wisdom? No, I preach Jesus Christ, the Savior." This is true in the sense that the task of Christian preaching is to proclaim the good news of Jesus Christ. In *The Apostolic Preaching and Its Developments*, C. H.

14. Parsons, "Wisdom and Natural Law," 288.

15. Hays, "Wisdom According to Paul," 113.

16. Parsons, "Wisdom and Natural Law," 289.

Dodd explores the origin of Christian preaching and insists that Christian preaching was originally not teaching but proclamation of the good news:

> The New Testament writers draw a clear distinction between preaching and teaching. . . . Teaching (*didaskein*) is in a large majority of cases ethical instruction. . . . Sometimes, especially in the Johannine writings, it includes the exposition of theological doctrine. Preaching, on the other hand, is the public proclamation of Christianity to the non-Christian world. The verb *keryssein* properly means "to proclaim." A *keryx* may be a town crier, an auctioneer, a herald, or anyone who lifts up his voice and claims public attention to some definite thing he has to announce.[17]

Dodd traces the development of apostolic preaching in the New Testament from the Pauline Epistles, through the Synoptic Gospels, to the Acts of the Apostles. The *kerygma* means the apostolic proclamation of salvation through the life, death, resurrection, and the second coming of Jesus Christ in a unique literary form. Those christological elements, according to Dodd, are "parts of the common Gospel" or the essence of the Christian gospel in the New Testament.[18] Through the *kerygma*, Paul and the authors of the Gospels identify Jesus as the wisdom of God,[19] i.e., the manifestation of God's nature—which is love. In other words, Jesus is not merely an enlightened sage or "a teacher of subversive wisdom,"[20] someone "memorable for his subversive parables and startling figures of speech."[21] Instead, he is "Wisdom incarnate" or "Emmanuel, God with us" (Matt 1:23).[22] As James Dunn describes it,

> to speak of Jesus as Wisdom incarnate may simply be to assert that God was present in and active through Jesus in a special way. . . . How would someone inspired to the nth degree differ in appearance and effect from one who was the incarnation of the inspiring power? . . . The language of adulation can move along a spectrum from inspiration towards incarnation. . . . Here, then, we have to recognize Jesus' own sense and affirmation that he himself was

17. Dodd, *Apostolic Preaching and Its Development*, 7.

18. Dodd, *Apostolic Preaching and Its Development*, 14; Lucy Rose uses the term *kerygma* as the synonym for "the gospel or the Word of God" in her book, *Sharing the Word*, 52, 54.

19. Cf., 1 Cor 1:24; Col 2:3.

20. Dunn, "Jesus," 78.

21. Barton, "Gospel Wisdom," 109.

22. Dunn, "Jesus," 78.

enacting something unusual, something distinctive, something final, the rue of God already manifested in its eschatological effectiveness through him. . . . To affirm that Jesus was a teacher of wisdom need not require us to deny that he was also in some sense Wisdom incarnate. . . . A Jesus who was simply a "teacher of wisdom" would claim his place within the tradition of Israel's great teachers. But, the Jesus who is remembered in the Synoptic tradition made a claim, both implicitly and explicitly, which transcended that of his precursors and which in the event could only find satisfactory expression in the evaluation of this Jesus as "Wisdom incarnate."[23]

Jesus as Wisdom incarnate represents the way in which a divine quality of love is humanly embodied: "'Where there is love, there is God' ('*Ubi caritas, Deus ibies*'). . . . 'Where there is wisdom, where there is justice, where there is integrity, there is God.'"[24] Anthony Kelly helps us understand the divine quality of love in the traditional Trinitarian language:

> God is originatively Love as Father, expressively Love as Son and communicatively Love as Spirit; three subjects in the one conscious infinite act of Being-in-Love. Each divine person has a distinct meaning in the self-constitution of the Divine Mystery; each is Love in a distinctive manner . . . the three are intelligible as Trinity only insofar as they manifest the Divine Mystery as Sheer Being-in-Love.[25]

Celia Deane-Drummond further states that the Trinitarian God is the source of both love and wisdom, because "the wisdom of God is never apart from Love. Similarly, Love is never apart from wisdom either."[26] Just as wisdom has an eschatological *telos*, so too the divine quality of love revealed in the wisdom of God in Jesus Christ is eschatological: "the *eschaton*, the final and decisive act of God, has already entered human experience,"[27] and the Spirit calls the community of faith to live an eschatological life that bears the "fruits of the Spirit" (Gal 5:20). The greatest gift of the Spirit is love (1 Cor 13), which is the root principle of all morality. God's love manifested in Jesus's life, death, and resurrection plays a positive role in renewing human

---

23. Dunn, "Jesus," 81, 87, 91, 92.

24. Moberly, "Solomon and Job," 17.

25. Kelly, cited in Deane-Drummond, *Creation Through Wisdom*, 129.

26. Deane-Drummond, *Creation Through Wisdom*, 129.

27. Dodd, *Apostolic Preaching and Its Development*, 34.

wisdom, and the movement of the Holy Spirit in communicating love in the human and natural world directs human wisdom toward the relationship of loving-kindness with other human beings and nature. Preaching Jesus, therefore, means preaching the wisdom of God, and preaching the wisdom of God means preaching a way of life of loving one another as God has demonstrated through the life, death, and resurrection of Jesus of Nazareth.

Yet, it is crucial for the preacher to remember what Dodd states in the concluding remarks of his book:

> do not suggest that the crude early formulation of the Gospel is our exclusive standard. It is only in the light of its development all through the New Testament that we learn how much is implied in it. . . . Gospels and epistles alike offer a field of study in which the labour of criticism and interpretation may initiate us into the "many-sided wisdom" which was contained in the apostolic Preaching, and make us free to declare it in contemporary terms to our own age.[28]

This statement encourages us to critically evaluate how the *kerygma* has been preached in the Christian church and to explore how this "many-sided wisdom" should be interpreted in order that it might be proclaimed relevantly in our contemporary context.

As Lucy Rose points out, most "kerygmatic" scholars and preachers tend to understand the *kerygma* as the timeless, unchangeable, and absolute "essential content" of the Christian gospel, or as "a set of statements and the saving activity of God," which automatically has the power to bring about the experience of divine encounter.[29] As a result, preaching the *kerygma* is often regarded as the event of God's "divine self-revelation"[30] to the listeners, with the preacher as God's "mouthpiece."[31] One of the contemporary examples of this kind of preaching is evangelical preaching in the United States, where the goal is to convert the listeners to Christianity, and in which the altar call is the crucial moment at the end of the sermon. Rose evaluates such a homiletical approach to the *kerygma* by raising five concerns: (1) the gap between preacher and the congregation from a "one-directional" communicational style;[32] (2) an unrealistic expectation that

28. Dodd, *Apostolic Preaching and Its Development*, 78.

29. Rose, *Sharing the Word*, 40.

30. Rose, *Sharing the Word*, 43.

31. Rose, *Sharing the Word*, 38.

32. Rose, *Sharing the Word*, 49.

every preaching moment should be a saving event;[33] (3) the focus on the individual listener, without considering the individual's relationship with the community;[34] (4) the uncertainty of the "unchanging, self-evident" nature of the *kerygma;* and (5) the impossibility of accomplishing the task of translating the *kerygma.*[35]

The alternative homiletical approach to the *kerygma* that I propose is to understand it from the perspective of wisdom and to interpret it with openness. Wisdom is open to insight from all disciplines, experiences, and cultures. In order to deepen understanding of the wisdom of God manifest in the *kerygma* and to make it accessible to humans, the preacher needs to open up to conversation with other religions, diverse human experiences, and the social sciences. Such interreligious and interdisciplinary studies provide hermeneutical space for creating new meaning for the *kerygma* that specifies the wisdom of God in a particular time and place. The sage in Proverbs illustrates the quest for wisdom through conversation with all parts of the world, by incorporating the best of wisdom materials from neighboring countries such as Egypt and Mesopotamia (Prov 22:17—24:22; 30:1; 31:1).

Paul's interpretation of the cross in 1 Cor 1:18—2:5 is another example of wisdom sought through openness. Through attentive listening to the particular historical and cultural context of the Corinthian church, Paul interprets the crucified Christ as the wisdom of God, which is "an eschatological gift and effect of the Holy Spirit."[36] The wisdom revealed on the cross is a radically different way of life in which racially, socially, and economically different people live together as "brothers and sisters" (1 Cor 1:26). This "eschatological reversal"[37] overturns worldly wisdom based on maintaining the status quo and calls the existing human community to transform itself into a new eschatological community, where people live with new values grounded in the nature of God. At this point, the wisdom of God revealed on the cross corresponds to the wisdom Jesus lived out

33. Rose, *Sharing the Word,* 50.

34. Rose, *Sharing the Word,* 51.

35. Rose, *Sharing the Word,* 55. In contemporary theological and homiletical discourse, theories of postliberal theology reflect this traditional understanding of the *kerygma* as the unchanging and absolute truth which requires only translation in diverse cultural contexts (cf., Campbell, *Preaching Jesus*). Rose's five concerns help us critically evaluate their theological and homiletical views on the *kerygma.*

36. Barton, "Gospel Wisdom," 104.

37. Hays, "Wisdom According to Paul," 116.

during his lifetime. It was not conventional, but eschatological, birthing a radically different world, i.e., a new age of the Spirit.

Our twenty-first-century multicultural and pluralistic world is similar to the first-century Greco-Roman world in some respects. Like the primitive churches in the New Testament, our contemporary churches are located in a global cultural environment of racism, classism, capitalism, sexism, and homophobia. One of the greatest challenges for Christian preachers is to seek the wisdom of God, not merely speculatively, but in the actual practice and experience of life. Christian believers need to listen to sermons that illuminate what it means to be truly human in our complex global context and what it means to free ourselves from our vested interests to see the common good of humanity. In the process of searching for wisdom, human wisdom and divine wisdom should intersect by working collaboratively without separation. More precisely, interdisciplinary studies with the social sciences, interfaith dialogue, and the critical analysis of human experiences help the preacher engage in conversation with the ancient formula of the *kerygma*. Through such interaction, the preacher becomes wise enough to see the world through the bifocal lens of both the human wisdom and the divine love, that we might seek a way of living together with others in love and solidarity in our particular historical and cultural context.

PREACHING AND SPIRITUAL PRACTICE

How might wisdom be effectively communicated through preaching? The answer to this question involves theological understanding of the nature and function of preaching, the image of the preacher, and the development of homiletical strategies. In the previous sections, the theological concept of wisdom and what it means to preach wisdom were explored. Moreover, the goal of preaching wisdom was elaborated so as to help listeners live wisely, by navigating their personal and communal life journeys as mature human beings in Christ, engaging in the rigor and discipline of love to transform themselves and their communities.

In order to achieve this goal, a wisdom homiletic understands the role of the preacher as a sage who is both a wisdom teacher and a spiritual director. McKenzie insists that the Christian preacher should be a wisdom teacher or a sage in order to help listeners shape the identity of their communities.[38] The identity of the Christian community represents

38. McKenzie, *Preaching Proverbs*, xxii.

its members' ways of seeing and being. The transformation of such identity does not happen only through lecturing on virtues. Instead, it requires the wisdom teacher to play a role beyond that of the lecturer.

Here, it is worth paying attention to what Paul says in 1 Cor 3:1–15. He describes his role as a teacher with the imagery of a nursing mother, a farmer, and a builder. In order to effectively teach the wisdom of God, he has played the role of a parent, especially "a breast-feeding mother" who provides the basics (1 Cor 3:1–4); a farmer (1 Cor 3:5–9), who is not one who simply works for a wage, but is a "soul-husbandman"; and "a wise master builder" who lays the foundation of the church with the gospel of the crucified Christ.[39] Moreover, in 1 Cor 4:14–21, Paul identifies himself as father and the members of the church as his children. Considering that the father's role in the first-century Jewish and Greco-Roman world is that of "the primary teacher of his children in educating and training them and that the requirement of his children is to honor and emulate the father,[40] the imagery of father denotes the parental relationship between the preacher and the listeners. The preacher as a wisdom teacher does not merely transmute knowledge about the wisdom of God, but cultivates true maturity in the members of the community that they might bear the fruits of the Spirit.

A wisdom homiletic also sees the preacher in the role of a spiritual director who helps the listeners discern the direction to maturity in the Spirit through spiritual practice. Spiritual practice in the Christian sense is the art of discerning the ways of God by attending to the inward and outward movements of the Holy Spirit, following the four virtues identified by McKenzie: we humble ourselves by being open to the movement of the Spirit, listen attentively to God and others by following the guidance of the Holy Spirit, control ourselves in response to the presence of the Spirit, and have courage to give a subversive voice to the world and live this out in our daily lives as the Spirit leads. The spiritual practice of seeking wisdom leads the preacher to ultimately turn into love, because, as Cahalan states, "the search for wisdom is entwined with the necessity for love,"[41] and "[c]harity cannot be acquired until discernment and humility are operative, for it is through these virtues that the heart is rid of selfish and evil intentions and charity emerges."[42]

39. White, *Where Is the Wise Man?*, 150–51.
40. White, *Where Is the Wise Man?*, 185.
41. Cahalan, "Spiritual Practices and the Search for a Wisdom Epistemology," 292.
42. Cahalan, "Spiritual Practices and the Search for a Wisdom Epistemology," 299.

In relation to spiritual practice, McKenzie reminds us that spiritual discipline is one of the common interests and practices of various religious traditions. She illustrates with the yogic disciplines of Hinduism, the mindfulness of Buddhism, and the prayer life of Islam.[43] In addition, it is useful to learn that Confucianism and Pure Land Buddhism practice quiet-sitting, recitation and memorization of the text, with copying and calligraphy as primary tools for understanding the profound meaning of humanity.[44] In Zen Buddhism, a *koan,* or paradoxical words, are also used for intuitive meditation and to experience enlightenment.[45]

Spiritual practice is an important aspect of Christianity, too. While contemporary Protestant churches tend to overlook its value, church history shows that in the early and medieval monastic life, spiritual practice was central in the search for wisdom. The practice of ancient Christian meditative reading known as *lectio divina* is one of the spiritual exercises for appreciating the text by reading slowly, prayerfully, and frequently, following the four steps of *lectio* (slow and attentive reading), *meditatio* (meditation through intuitive imagination), *oratio* (prayer as conversation with God), and *contemplatio* (an experience of the grace of God by emptying oneself).[46]

The spiritual hermeneutics I propose in *Preaching the Presence of God* is another exercise in spirituality. It is the art of seeking wisdom through the integration of the ancient methods of meditation and the contemporary critical methods of biblical interpretation. Through the seven stages of the hermeneutical process,[47] the preacher follows the lead of the Holy Spirit and engages in dialogue with the text and with listeners to reflect on a meaning of the text that is relevant to contemporary listeners.

Just as spiritual hermeneutics uses dialogue as the key in searching for wisdom, so the wisdom homiletic takes it as the major homiletical approach. Dialogue requires the open-mindedness of preacher and the

43. McKenzie, *Hear and Be Wise,* 76.

44. Kim, *Preaching the Presence of God,* 80, 82.

45. Kim, *Preaching the Presence of God,* 83.

46. Kim, *Preaching the Presence of God,* 95.

47. Kim, *Preaching the Presence of God,* 98–101: (1) Prayerful preparation; (2) text selection based on pastoral sensibility; (3) attentive reading through intuitive imagination; (4) critical understanding with the help of biblical resources; (5) sensitive listening to the reality of the listeners, locally and globally; (6) dynamic interaction between the world of the text and that of the context; and (7) theological reflection on the meaning attained through the six stages above from the Christian eschatological perspective.

listeners and mutual respect between them. In order to have genuine dialogue, it is essential for them to open their minds in humility and listen attentively, following the lead of the Holy Spirit, to the point of converging their words of wisdom.

Dialogue is normally regarded as a verbal exchange. Yet, the dialogue of silence is a powerful spiritual practice. In Confucianism and Buddhism, silence is valued as "a moment through which thoughts and feelings occur from emptiness."[48] In preaching, as I have emphasized, silence between words and sentences in pauses, waiting, and imagination is "a moment of active listening, reflecting things deeply, and grasping meanings intuitively."[49] The preacher may initiate dialogue with imagery, metaphor, sayings, and stories, and invite the listeners to a dialogue using verbal and nonverbal forms.

In relation to the use of language in the wisdom homiletic, it is worth paying attention to David Bland, who values "a memorable quality" of the proverb in communication—"brevity and wit." According to Bland, "a short sentence based on a long experience" or "a maximum of meaning with a minimum of words"[50] has the power to appeal aesthetically to both heart and mind.[51] Such language provides both preacher and listeners with space for meditation and stirs the imagination to envision a new way of life.

The wisdom homiletic as spiritual practice is an ongoing dialogue between the preacher and the listeners, between the text and the context, and between human wisdom and divine wisdom. Wisdom attained through spiritual practice is a gift of the Holy Spirit that has the power to shape and reshape personal and communal identity. Just as the search for wisdom is eschatological, so the wisdom homiletic is eschatological, an effort to search for a direction toward the eschatological community.

48. Kim, *Preaching the Presence of God*, 110.

49. Kim, *Preaching the Presence of God*, 111.

50. Bland, *Proverbs and the Formation of Character*, 82.

51. Bland, *Proverbs and the Formation of Character*, 83.

6

Ephobounto gar

Fear, Wisdom, and the Homiletical-Theological Task of
Speaking Gospel in Crisis Situations

DAVID SCHNASA JACOBSEN

> Succinctly put, homiletical theology is the exercise of practical wisdom.
> —Alyce McKenzie

ONE OF THE MOST important features of Alyce McKenzie's contribution to
the field is her insistence on drawing deeply on the traditions of wisdom for
preaching and relating that steadfastly to the work of homiletics as practical
theology. Professor McKenzie's work in this regard has been both deep and
wide. I wish here to engage this significant part of her research agenda by
carrying it forward.

I am relating the two, wisdom traditions and the notion of homiletical
theology as practical wisdom, in an admittedly arbitrary way: the importance of the "fear of the Lord" as the *beginning* of all wisdom (Prov 9:10) and
the problem of traumatic "fear" posed by preaching in crisis situations.[1] I
do not wish to muddle the difference between theological and anthropological fear, but I am convinced that the exercise of practical wisdom in

1. I first developed this paper in connection with a paper presented at the 2018 meeting of *Societas Homiletica*, whose theme was "Fearing God in a Fear-Filled World," held
at Duke Divinity School in early August. I wish to thank my international colleagues in
homiletics whose responses helped to improve this paper along the way!

the midst of crisis situations is important for preacher and homiletician alike. The path I wish to take to help unpack these issues is therefore both scriptural and theological. I begin by describing the odd, traumatic ending of Mark's Gospel in the stunningly brief resurrection material of 16:1–8 that end with the Greek words "*ephobounto gar*," or, "for they were afraid." I then turn to Serene Jones's work in *Trauma and Grace* to reread the Markan ending in light of trauma theory. In the final part of this article I turn to the problem of preaching in situations of crisis and propose what I hope are suitably wise and fitting theologically laden practices, so that even the homiletical-theological task of preaching in crisis is itself understood as an exercise in practical wisdom.

FEARING THE END WITH MARK'S GOSPEL

The Gospel of Mark ends disturbingly in the Greek New Testament. According to text-critical scholars, the Gospel's most likely ending is at 16:8 with the women at the tomb running away, saying nothing, "for they were afraid." The ending surprises us because it does not appear to us to be how a gospel should end. As contemporary preachers, we may sometimes be tempted to read Mark in light of Matthew, Luke, and perhaps even John, all of whom have more than just an "empty tomb" scene and an expression of fear, but include commissions, appearances, and any number of postresurrection narratives of the risen Jesus. This reception history from the canon all the way to today is precisely what makes it so hard for us to grasp Mark's uniqueness here. If indeed Mark is the oldest of the four Gospels, the truth of this unique ending seems even more startling given its place in the tradition. Mark, the oldest Gospel, does not wrap up his story with a happy ending at 16:8, but concludes with the puzzling words about the women who told no one anything, *ephobounto gar*, for they were *afraid*.

A Gospel ending with fear does not seem to have been satisfying to the tradition. If the synoptic hypothesis is correct, Matthew and Luke intervened fairly early in the process by adding to Mark's bare-bones ending of the empty tomb tradition. What perhaps is even more telling, however, is the way that subsequent manuscripts of Mark seem to be trying to correct Mark's mysterious ending. For this reason, readers of English translations of Mark that honor this manuscript tradition add bracketed material as well as verses 9–20, called the "intermediate ending" and the "longer ending," respectively. It appears that the manuscript tradition itself struggled with Mark's ending which features the verb "to fear" and concludes, un-characteristically, with the conjunction *gar*.

Contemporary interpreters have tried to work around Mark's fearful ending in their own ways. Some argue that a happier ending is implied. Since we know that the Gospel got to us readers, we can trust that the women eventually did the right thing and actually told the disciples so the Gospel's gospel could be carried forward. Other interpreters focus on the reader's role and argue that where characters in the narrative itself fear and fail, the readers of Mark's Gospel have insight that the characters in the narrative do not possess and therefore have the task of completing the narrative laid in their laps—the readers finish the narrative that most of the main characters fail to comprehend. Here, the knowing reader, now an insider to the Markan narrative, provides in a reader-response fashion a more appropriate ending to Mark's Gospel.

The point here is not to inventory all the possible endings of Mark, happy or not. The intent is, rather, to identify the constructive homiletical-theological problem at the heart of Christian faith in a time of profound fear, grief, and perhaps even trauma. In fact, I wish to show how this prob-lem in the tradition emerges as an occasion that helps us think about our task as wise homiletical theologians and the fearful context in which early Christian texts struggle to speak from the beginning.

RECALLING THE BEGINNING OF MARK'S GOSPEL

One reason that Mark's ending is so strange has to do with the careful framing at the very beginning of the Gospel. Mark 1:1 functions like a su-perscription for the work: "The beginning of the gospel of Jesus Christ." Mark's Gospel may be mostly a story. Here at the beginning, however, the Gospel indicates that it is about the "gospel," *tou euangeliou* and aligns that gospel with Jesus Christ.[2] Mark signals clearly to readers that his Gospel is about the gospel. By the end of the introductory material in 1:14–15, Mark returns to the theme of the gospel, but now places the word in Je-sus' mouth as he emerges from his wilderness temptation triumphant and ready to begin his ministry of healing, exorcism, and feeding. The gospel in verses 14–15, which Jesus announces, is now specifically called "the gospel of God," and is aligned with Jesus' proclamation of the divine reign. From

2. I use the capitalized word Gospel to designate Mark's work; and the lowercase word "gospel" to describe the theological message that Mark's Gospel is concerned with.

the beginning, Mark's Gospel names the gospel as both Jesus Christ and the gospel of God's reign.

It is the juxtaposition of this clear beginning and muddled ending that raises the key question: Why does the first of the Gospels make such a strong opening claim and conclude with a confusing, tragic ending? How can a Gospel about the gospel end like this?

A DEEPER WISDOM: SERENE JONES
AND THE ENDS OF THE GOSPEL

In light of this very theological way of putting the question, it becomes quite interesting to look at the work of Serene Jones in her book, *Trauma and Grace*.[3] Jones likewise notes the disruptive ending of the Gospel of Mark, but rereads it through embodied experiences of trauma.[4] Trauma does not admit easy endings; in fact, trauma has the tendency to return. Similarly, in Mark the awful event of the cross is not resolved in the brief references to resurrection in 16:1–8. It is a troubling, unfinished Gospel of the gospel.

Jones first notes that the word "end" has two meanings. It speaks of course to the notion of a conclusion—that is true. But the language of "end" in English carries another meaning of theological weight: end as *purpose*. In light of this, Jones asks what is the end (purpose) of this Gospel about the gospel of the cross? Such purpose, she notes, is not just a once-and-for-all reality, but one that can and does break into our lives this side of our ultimate end (the first sense). In this way, it is almost analogous to an understanding of healing that does not limit itself to a completed act, but an ongoing one that emerges from time to time in the present. In this way, Jones asks a crucial question: "how [might we] tell stories about violence that . . . bear witness to God's forming grace and mercy?"[5]

---

3. Jones, *Trauma and Grace*, 87–96. What follows is my summary of this portion of Jones's work.

4. Trauma theory has begun to impact North American homiletics in profound ways. Dr. Kimberly Wagner's 2018 Emory dissertation deals with preaching, trauma theory, and the problem of gun violence in the US, see "From the Depths: Preaching in Wake of Mass Violent Trauma." In a regional Ted Talk from 2017, Boston University homiletics PhD student Nikki Young offers a summary of the impact of "collective trauma" in and across cultures: https://www.youtube.com/watch?v=4a7Ai2_JIoI&list=PLsRNoUx8w3r P2RrF1Os6CbDhfudvRMRyR&index=2.

5. Jones, *Trauma and Grace*, 86.

Along the way, Jones notes that the fear expressed in the final verse, *ephobounto gar*, is not the only testimony to its reality. The alarm that the women experience, and from which the angel tries to dissuade them, is also a verb of great fear (*exethambêthêsan* in 16:5, 6). The women's fear is thus such that they are frightened into speechlessness. This, for Jones, tends to underline the importance of Mark's missing ending for those experiencing trauma. Mark's Gospel of the gospel has no ordered closure; nor does it press toward some sort of compensatory understanding. It ends in its own unraveled way. It fails to make theological meaning in any of the senses we would expect.

Jones notes two ways that this actually fits the situation of those who have been traumatized, for whom fear is a returning reality without easy closure. A narrative that has such holes in it, a narrative that does not press toward an ordered ending, actually fits the experience of those who have undergone trauma. Trauma, in this sense, inhabits the body, its muscle memory, and is not easily disposed of by feats of narrative closure. Such open-ended narrative may thereby offer a more fitting aesthetic. Second, if the nature of this trauma is to alarm and terrify into silence, perhaps an unusual narrative like Mark's opens up a space for renewed agency on the part of those who live in such fear. Jones even goes on to emphasize that Mark's ending could possibly open up into performances of unspoken gestures—indeed, perhaps silent gesture is the only way to open up meaning in the face of such fear.

AN EXERCISE OF HOMILETICAL THEOLOGY FOR PREACHING IN CRISIS SITUATIONS

For me, this kind of constructive-theological work goes beyond the exegetical questions surrounding the interpretation of Mark's ending. The question with which Jones wrestles is, at heart, a profound issue of what I call homiletical theology. Homiletical theology views preaching as a place where theology is done. It is, as Alyce McKenzie notes, "an exercise of practical wisdom."[6] For those who preach in situations of crisis, such moments confront preachers in ever-new ways, and in ever-new contexts.[7] What do

6. McKenzie, "Company of Sages," 88.

7. Homileticians in North America have begun to wrestle with crisis preaching as a specific preaching moment: Joseph Jeter Jr's book *Crisis Preaching* and Samuel Proctor's *Preaching about Crises in the Community* are excellent examples of this. Ron Allen has

preachers say when situations unravel and escape any attempt at the theological ordering that is a happy ending? What is the gospel for those moments? Homiletical theologians in such moments will draw on the riches of Scripture, but they will also need to name in the midst of this what are actually local silences, fears, and terrors that the Scriptures sometimes only intimate. How might we speak and gesture toward gospel in the face of this situational unraveling?

At the center of what I call homiletical theology is a confessional-correlational process that includes what André Resner calls a "working gospel."[8] In a situation of crisis, which we are proposing to relate to Jones's reflections on cross and resurrection in trauma, preachers as theologians bring into conversation gospel and context. Part of what Jones offers, I believe, is a sense of the asymmetry of preaching gospel in such crisis situations: the limits of understanding and knowledge, the halting and unfinished nature of the conversation crisis engenders, and the proximity of all this to bodies in whom fear and trauma are inscribed. Strange as it may sound, I think that Jones helps to reframe the task of preaching in situations of crisis in at least three helpful ways.

1. "Returning" to a Theology of the Cross

Jones highlights the importance of "returning" to trauma and relates it to the uniquely Markan take on cross and resurrection. I am proposing that we take the notion of returning and use it in reference to a theology of the cross that both exercises its critical function and yet is in itself revisable in crisis preaching. Luther's notion of a theology of the cross differs somewhat from more recent struggles over the cross chiefly in relation to atonement

---

named the theological significance of preaching in such moments more broadly in his work *Preaching the Topical Sermon*. I am doing something similar in picking up elements of David Buttrick's "situational preaching" in relation to his "preaching in the mode of praxis," in *Homiletic: Moves and Structures* while relating it to Ed Farley's work on relating a theology of gospel to practice and unpacking the notion of a "hermeneutic of situations," both of which are treated in his *Practicing Gospel*. I have ventured my own thoughts on preaching in crisis situations in connection with my work with Robert Kelly in *Kairos Preaching*, 124–50.

8. André Resner developed the notion of "working gospel" in an insightful article, "Reading the Bible for Preaching the Gospel," 223. Since then, Resner has expanded his approach to a more explicitly apocalyptic understanding of gospel in *Living In-Between*.

theory. For Luther, a theology of the cross "calls a thing what it really is."[9] It relates much more closely to a theology of revelation in a kind of cruciform key, as Douglas John Hall describes it.[10] In Luther's formulation it parts ways with a theology of glory that associates divine revelation with exalted forms of human power, and looks instead at weakness—assuming that God reveals Godself in the cross *sub contrario*. Precisely as a critical principle, a theology of the cross may just be wise for responding to the trauma-centered theology that Jones articulates. At the same time, there is even with a theology of the cross a reductionistic tendency that struggles to see ways in which cross and power intersect and thus invite further critical revision for our homiletical-theological task of speaking gospel in crisis. Deanna Thompson and other feminist theologians make a case for a revision of a theology of the cross in light of women's suffering.[11] More recently, James Cone argues that the Black community's experience of lynching both critiques and enlarges that theology by juxtaposing the cross with the lynching tree.[12]

The homiletical goal is not to apply cross language willy-nilly. Instead it invites preachers into practical wisdom in the form of an act of discernment to explore both how the cross refuses the evasions that misname and thus erase trauma, as well as to see how an experience of trauma itself pushes back on our preaching of the cross. A view of "returning" to a theology of the cross may just permit preaching in crisis situations to connect more deeply to the embodied contradictions of the tradition in a way that allows preachers and hearers to bear halting, difficult witness to one another.

2. God Preached and God Not Preached

An important piece of the exercise of wisdom for preaching in situations of crisis is to acknowledge what human beings do and do not know. Trauma, as Jones points out, has a way of leaving those impacted silenced and terrorized. Crisis, likewise, opens up the possibility *in situ* that we cannot yet

9. Martin Luther deals with this notion in the Heidelberg Disputation. Gerhard Foerde treats it in great detail in his book *On Being a Theologian of the Cross*.

10. Douglas John Hall offers a uniquely Canadian perspective on the antitriumphalism of Luther's theology of the cross in North America in *The Cross in Our Context*.

11. Some recent examples are Solberg, *Compelling Knowledge*; Trelstad, *Cross Examinations*; and Thompson, *Crossing the Divide*.

12. Cone, *Cross and the Lynching Tree*.

say all that might be said. It becomes a moment where preachers need to be honest about what they know and do not know. "For now," says Paul, "we see through a glass, darkly" (1 Cor 13:12 KJV).

In light of these contextual and situational realities, Luther's notion of God preached and not preached may offer a partial way of thinking through the limits of our homiletical-theological task. In response to the speculative tendencies of some late medieval theology, Luther is careful to distinguish between what we can say about God and what we cannot.[13] Holding tightly to divine mystery, Luther recognizes that God cannot simply be explained by what we know and can say. In the face of this mystery, however, Luther holds to the notion of God's disclosure in Christ, to what we can know and say about God. For Luther, our talk of God must acknowledge its limits.

Although going beyond Luther's formulation, an appreciation as well for the mystery of otherness that we encounter in humanity in all its diversity should give occasion for homiletical-theological modesty when preaching in situations of crisis. Jones reminds us that the traumatized can find themselves retraumatized in Christian preaching. Is there a theological-anthropological corollary to Luther's notion, now enlarged by what we learn about our differences in a world where the exclusion of trauma is arbitrarily applied across populations? Perhaps a more nuanced, wise approach to humanity in crisis can help us see proclamation as not simply a reinscribing of the tradition, regardless of our fears, but a more fragmentary offering that freely acknowledges what we know, and what we do not know, in the face of crisis.

3. Preaching in Crisis: From Deductive and Inductive to "Abductive" Invention

Preaching sometimes structures its discourse by means of inventional logics that help to order life in light of gospel. Models of deductive and inductive preaching have, at various points, vied for influence, especially in the late-twentieth-century North American pulpit.[14] However, neither the

13. You can find a helpful summary of Luther's thought again with the work of Gerhard Foerde in *Theology Is for Proclamation*, 15–17.

14. A helpful summary of these in situational or topical preaching is found in Ron Allen's work, *Preaching the Topical Sermon*. While not advocating for any particular inventional logic for preaching, Professor McKenzie's own work on homiletical theology as an exercise in practical wisdom argues that it represents a kind of sapiential hermeneutic in an inductive mode ("Company of Sages," 87–102). It may be that preaching in crisis

inductive nor deductive path may be the most useful for the kind of crisis preaching that experiences of trauma may be helping us to revision.

American pragmatist philosopher Charles Peirce mentions a third possibility, an "abductive" logic or mode of inference, and thus adds it to the traditional Aristotelian deductive and inductive modes. Peirce uses the term to signify a kind of reasoning that ventures a hypothesis and tests it. For Peirce, abductive reasoning joins inductive and deductive as the third kind of logical inference. Of course, some have critiqued Peirce for including abductive reasoning, especially since it appears to be more a form of explanation of a theory already held. For Peirce, however, abduction does not belong to justifying an already ventured theory, but is rather a form of discovery capable of generating new theories.

Admittedly, the rather abstract language of logical inference in relation to homiletical invention does not, at first blush, seem readily usable for the fearful, traumatic situations of crisis we have been assuming. However, its generative approach may just prove helpful for a homiletical theology that views its task constructively! Using Jones's work, therefore, I wish to flesh out a further meaning of Peirce's abduction not only as an idealized form of reasoning, but a more metaphorically embodied gesture in view of the admitted shattering of meaning in a situation. Jones envisions an embodied gesture as the "end" (in the second sense) of Mark's Gospel in interpretation.[15] My goal is to show how abductive invention in a sermon might embody metaphorically a way about preaching gospel in moments of public crisis.

One reason I particularly revel in the use of "abductive" for this type of reasoning is its secondary use as a term in relation to muscle movement. Abductor muscles are muscles in the body that enable movement away from the median of the body. If, say, you stand with your arms at your side and proceed to draw (-duct) them up away from your body (ab-) to take a cruciform shape, for example, you would, biomechanically speaking, be engaging in a kind of abduction.

I have therefore fleshed out a kind of playful revision of the term of inference, "abductive," to describe a kind of "embodied" theological structure for situational preaching in crises. Although abductive reasoning acknowledges its all-too-fragmentary knowledge, nonetheless it aims provisionally

---

sometimes leads us to the edge of the deductive and inductive logics by which we live and come to an understanding about a situation.

15. Jones, *Trauma and Grace*, 94–95.

to gesture toward truth—even if only piecemeal—as a kind of hypothesis. To put this into sermonic context, I would like to imagine an analogous situation to help embody this kind of practical wisdom at work in abductive invention.

> In the midst of X (facts of crisis) there is Y (God not preached) we do not know.[16]
>
> However, we can hold on to Z (God preached).
>
> Therefore, Z points us forward in the midst of ambiguity.

The logical structure above on its own is conceivable given our reflections, but it is its truly embodied inventional counterpart below that makes it *plausible* as a homiletical-theological exercise in wisdom in a *traumatic*, crisis situation. There are, no doubt, some things in moments of trauma that the body knows: the knot in the stomach, the desire to step back, or a feeling of detachment or numbness in an almost-out-of-body experience (think of how preaching in a crisis can make preachers feel tongue-tied!). Metaphorically, then, I liken the abductive kind of homiletical-theological inference to a sermon that:

> *names the shattered glass in a situation,*
> *picks up a shard,*
> *and juxtaposing it bodily holds it up to the light.*

Such abductive preaching in crisis is difficult in that it takes place precisely in the midst of broken glass and vulnerable bodies. But crisis preaching is nonetheless a place where we are called and empowered to name gospel as a risked hypothesis in our bodies. In this way, to paraphrase Prof. McKenzie, homiletical theology may just also be an occasion for the bodily exercise of practical wisdom.

---

16. This first step is important not only for acknowledging the facts of a difficult situation, but our realization about what we do *not* know about God in relation to it. Perhaps, with Socrates as portrayed in Plato's *Apology*, we can argue that wisdom also consists in knowing what we do not know.

7

"Simpletons, Scoffers, and Fools"
Roles Wise Preachers Should Avoid

JOHN C. HOLBERT

WHEN THINKING OF MY former colleague and now long-time friend, Alyce McKenzie, it is inevitable that the book of Proverbs springs to mind. She has spent much of her scholarly and preaching life attempting in richly creative ways to illuminate that literature that has too often played only a very small role in the repertoire of most preachers, even among those, like me, who relish texts from the Hebrew Bible. I am certainly not naive when it comes to the small number of lovers of the First Testament for preaching; I often imagine that a meeting of such a club would find an antiquated phone booth more than adequate. But since phone booths have in the main gone the way of the dodo, we may need to move such a meeting to a musty church basement room, with out-of-tune piano in the corner, the better not to pollute those numerous exclusive lovers of the New Testament, who will be up in the sanctuary communing with their many friends. No need to raise your hands; your numbers are legion, if I may employ a metaphor from your own beloved text.

Still, even I must admit that Proverbs has seldom for me moved to the top of the homiletical charts. Too many juicy narratives to plumb, too many fine poems, too many legal traditions worthy of a closer look. But

Proverbs? "Freeze-dried" truths, as they might be called, or pithy, pungent, and prickly, one might say. It is hardly my intent in this brief essay to prove to you that Proverbs can be a wonderful resource for any preacher, though Alyce has tried to prove that to be true,[1] and I heartily agree with her, though I admit my agreement is rather more in the mind than actively in the pulpit; quite frankly, I have rarely used the book in my own preaching. I am in this essay more interested in what the collection of Proverbs has to say about us preachers, rather than in the content of what we try to say, and more specifically what it claims are the chief dangers for those who regularly open their mouths for proclamation, risking speech on behalf of God, itself perhaps the act of a simpleton fool opening herself up to derisive scoffers, if I may employ the words of the moment.

It is easy to demonstrate that the dangers for preachers are myriad, leading to laughable, if not fatal, results. Alyce and I wrote a book together some years ago called *What Not to Say*,[2] wherein we attempted to demonstrate from our own preaching and from the preaching we have heard from our many students over the years any number of pitfalls that can sink a sermon in the depths of the sea or at least deep enough to deprive both preacher and hearer of the oxygen needed to sustain life. I think the book is still worth reading; I can imagine Alyce thinks so, too.

In this article I want to focus more specifically on three things the author(s) of Proverbs warn against, three states of being that he/she urges readers to avoid at all costs. Though the warning is for any reader, preacher or no, I will attempt to demonstrate how cogent the warnings are for modern preachers in particular. The book of Proverbs holds up three kinds of persons that are familiar, indeed common, in the culture of the writer, but each of them must be eschewed if the reader/preacher is to remain genuinely faithful to God and to self, as well as to be wisely successful in the preaching life.

A verse containing all three dangerous states occurs early in the book, Prov 1:22. Here is the NRSV translation:

> How long, O simple ones, will you love being simple?
> How long will scoffers delight in their scoffing
>   and fools hate knowledge?

---

1. McKenzie, *Preaching Proverbs* and McKenzie, *Hear and Be Wise*.
2. Holbert and McKenzie, *What Not to Say*.

The verse exists at the center of the call of Lady Wisdom to those whom she is convinced are in desperate need of the wares she has to offer. Apparently, the three kinds of persons she enumerates, those we will concern ourselves with here, are those in most need.

The first is that much-maligned "simpleton." In our time the word is little used, but if it is, it implies a naïve person, one easily led, one lacking the sense to live effectively and safely in the world. Perhaps the fictional Forrest Gump may be classed among the simpletons. However, because his status as simpleton results finally in his endearing ease and success in multiple situations, he is not an example of what the word means to the wisdom writers of the Bible. To the contrary, *Pathah* or *pathi*, the words usually translated as "simpleton" in the NRSV, refer to a person who lacks something important and presents some shortcoming that exists as immaturity or a limited understanding, leading to a less-than-successful life. Therefore, the "simpleton" is in desperate need of wisdom, what Lady Wisdom in Proverbs offers to all who would hear her. Whatever the definition of wisdom, it is the antidote to a malarial case of being a simpleton.

Some examples make the point. Prov 9:13 states that the simpleton (here a "foolish woman") "knows nothing," and covers her ignorance by being "loud." Prov 20:19 describes the simpleton as both a "gossip" and a "babbler." Prov 14:15 suggests that the simpleton "believes everything," because, according to Prov 1:4, he lacks "shrewdness" as well as "knowledge and prudence." Prov 7:7 announces straightforwardly that the simpleton "lacks sense."

The lengthy lament of Lady Wisdom at Prov 1:20–33 reinforces the vast dangers to the simpleton who refuses her admonishment. Though she "cries out in the street" (Prov 1:20) and directly addresses "the simple ones" (Prov 1:22) in her cries, because they "love being simple" and like "fools hate knowledge" (Prov 1:22), they refuse to pay any attention to her. As a result, they "have ignored all my counsel," have completely disregarded "my reproof" (Prov 1:25), and will therefore "eat the fruit of their ways" and "be stuffed with their own devices" (Prov 1:31). The disasters awaiting the unreformed simpleton are summarized at Prov 1:32–33: "Waywardness kills the simple; the complacency of fools destroys them. But those who listen to me [Lady Wisdom] will be secure and will live at ease with no dread of disaster."

The figure of the simpleton in other places of the Hebrew Bible narrates the results of such refusals to become something other than simple.

Delilah, that antithesis of Lady Wisdom, tries again and again to make the fool of her brutish lover, Samson, and finally succeeds by wheedling from him the secret of his vast strength, then gives him one of history's most famous haircuts, which leads to his blinding by the Philistines and ultimately to all their deaths in the shocking destruction of the temple of Dagon (Judg 14–16).

In the terrible story of Jeremiah, the lonely and abused prophet, the word we are discussing extends its meaning to "deceive" or "seduce." The simpleton has now become the plaything of YHWH, has opened himself up to YHWH's deception and seduction (Jer 20:7). Jeremiah as simpleton finds himself the target of the all-powerful God who, the prophet believes, has tricked him into the prophetic life, a life filled with anguish and rejection. Jeremiah has answered the call of his God, however reluctantly (see Jer 1:4–19), and the result has been a solitary and appalling existence. In other words, Jeremiah's simple life of faith in YHWH has led him to abuse by that God. This sad story employs the word "simpleton" in a clearly theological way, but its use has taken a very dark turn, and YHWH has used Jeremiah's designation as simpleton to attack him, at least as far as the prophet can judge. This dark side of YHWH is repeated in Ezek 14:9, where the prophet says quite pointedly, "If a prophet is deceived and speaks a word, I, YHWH, have deceived that prophet, and I will stretch out my hand against him and will destroy him from the midst of my people." This verse states with a terrible clarity that YHWH at times deceives followers, leading them to speak words of deception, and then this same YHWH destroys the speakers for speaking the deception that YHWH placed within them! This astonishing claim cries out for theological reflection, but that reflection must be saved for another time. What is important for us is that in these two prophetic cases, being a simpleton has become the way to destruction and death at the hands of YHWH. The conclusion to draw is that being a simpleton, and persisting in that state, is a sure path to doom, whether caused by YHWH or not.

What may a modern preacher take from all this ancient talk of the dangers of being and remaining a simpleton? Robert Alter, in his engaging translation and commentary on the Proverbs,[3] translates our word as "dupe." I suggest that this reading may come closer to what the ancient writer had in mind by warning us against this particular trait, a trait that apparently infected not a few people in his own time. A "dupe" is a rube,

3. Alter, *Wisdom Books*, 193–334.

an easy mark, a person willing to accept anything and everything without thinking and without question. The dupe is a victim, a sucker, a target, what we call a fall guy. He/she is unthinking, inexperienced, gullible.

How may a twenty-first-century preacher fall into the trap of the dupe? Whenever a preacher, charged with proclaiming the word of God to a congregation, called to speak truth into a world too often devoid of truth, fails to open herself to more than a simple repetition of ideas gleaned from suspect or foolish sources (the internet in its myriad and too-often-unsupported babble, other sources of so-called "news" that is less news than entertainment, or any number of online blogs and chat rooms), she is a dupe, subject to the mouthing of nonsense, since she herself possesses no real sense to discern or to struggle to uncover what is truth and what is merely conjecture or hearsay or downright idiocy. Our social media sources can do many things, but delivering clear and well-thought-out truth is not one of them. The preacher as dupe becomes presumptuous, arrogant, impudent, and conceited in her ignorance and can be no worthy guide for those she is called to serve.

I had a student once who upon graduation from my seminary, vowed too loudly to me on that day that he would, "never read a book of theology again." I am certain he kept that vow throughout the course of his ministry. I suggest that he is the very model of the dupe, a mountebank proclaiming his own brand of "gospel truth," unaffected by the deeper call of Lady Wisdom to seek genuine wisdom through hard work and study and thus to fill his sermons with rich biblical sense and serious engagement with facts and reason. The preacher-as-dupe is far too common in twenty-first-century pulpits.

And that sad reality of the dupe leads us to the second of our words that the NRSV translates as "scoffer," another brand of person who has closed his ears to the call of Lady Wisdom. This reading is more traditional than it is an accurate rendering of the Hebrew. Ps 1:1 may be the most famous use of the noun form, based on the verb *lits.* "Happy (blessed) are those who do not follow the advice of the wicked, or take the path that sinners tread, or sit in the seat of scoffers." The three parallel nouns, "wicked," "sinners," and "scoffers," are set in opposition to those who "delight in the Torah of YHWH," who meditate on the Torah day and night" (Ps 1:2). The first two negative nouns are quite common and quite general in application; "wicked" and "sinners" occur throughout the Hebrew Bible as designations of any number of acts deemed inappropriate and dangerous for those who claim to be followers of God. However, the third term, "scoffers," is less clear. In addition, it is used in the tradition far less frequently, fewer than ten times. Because of that fact, to fix the precise meaning of the term is not easy.

English "scoffing" presents the image of one who scorns, a loudmouth know-it-all who reveals her anger and rejection of an idea through speech. We are said to scoff at something or someone when we desire to belittle or deride an idea or person that we find detestable or foolish. Scoffing is by its very nature furious speech. There is no clear indication in the uses of this word in Hebrew that speech is the essence of the action it refers to. In none of the places where the verb/noun occur can it be said that speaking is necessarily involved. A glance at Ps 119:51; Prov 3:34; 9:12; 14:9 (a very difficult Hebrew text, as NRSV footnote suggests), 19:28; Isa 28:12; and Hos 7:5 make the point. Only at Prov 19:28 could it be inferred that scoffing involves speech: "A worthless witness mocks (scoffs) at justice, and the mouth of the wicked devours iniquity." The juxtaposition of "mouth" and "mocks" in the two lines could indicate speech, but hardly necessarily.

It seems safer to conclude that "scoffing" in these texts suggests no specific verbal fault, but rather indicts the scoffer as "presumptuous, arrogant, conceited, or impudent"[4] as a state of being rather than a loudmouth talker. However, the fact that the poet of Ps 1 classes the scoffer with those who are sinners and wicked makes it clear that being a scoffer, whatever it means specifically, is no good thing to be. Far better to delight in the Torah than to find one's seat with scoffers!

Perhaps the scoffer might be contrasted with the dupe in the following way: the dupe opens himself to being led into foolishness and stupidity, because he has no real knowledge of the truth, and becomes thereby a presumptuous and arrogant person, inured to the call of Lady Wisdom, while the scoffer then may be the result of the idiocy of the simpleton, the dupe. Hence, the dupe inevitably becomes the scoffer, characterized by stupid arrogance and rash and unfounded conceit. Dupes and scoffers, who claim to be preachers, speak loudly and forcefully, but have no knowledge on which to base their speaking. They are mountebanks, blowhards who mouth words that sound impressive and seek to be persuasive, but whose significance has no basis in the truths of wisdom.

4. Rudolf Mosis in Botterweck, Ringgren, and Fabry, *Theological Dictionary of the Old Testament*, 12:166.

I think of the so-called friends of Job, especially his first friend, Eliphaz. This man from Teman, who has supposedly come to "comfort" his friend in his deep distress, instead skewers Job rapaciously with words and phrases that seek to destroy the sinner rather than aid his reentry into his lost community. Eliphaz takes one look at Job on his trash heap, surrounded by fish heads and watermelon rinds, and concludes immediately that he must be the foulest sinner in the land. After all, Eliphaz is thoroughly convinced that God rewards the righteous and punishes the wicked, and the sight of Job can only mean that God has punished him for some terrible evil. Thus, his pious-sounding phrases: "Think now, Job; who that was innocent ever perished? Where were the upright ever cut off?" "As I have seen it, those who plow iniquity, and sow trouble, always reap the same" (Job 4:7–8). These may sound on the surface like long-hallowed truths of deep wisdom, but since we know from the first two chapters of the story that Job himself is "upright" (Job 1:1, 8), Eliphaz's "truths" in this case are far from the truth. Though Eliphaz goes on at great length and with considerable rotund eloquence to class Job with the sinners, at least as he understands sin, in the end his sermon becomes cruel and ludicrous, concluding with his call for Job to "hear, and know all this for yourself" (Job 5:27)! Eliphaz, like all mountebanks, hardly expects any response from his hearers save applause and acquiescence. When Job proceeds to reject his sermon with increasingly angry words of his own, the most shocked and horrified person in the drama is Eliphaz.[5]

Eliphaz did not die a long time ago, but instead continues to inhabit many of our twenty-first-century pulpits. Eliphaz is the epitome of the dupe and the scoffer, employing stale, secondhand ideas as if they were the only ideas that count. Eliphaz needs to turn his ears to Lady Wisdom to receive a spirit of humility and openness, the better to sharpen and hone his thoughts and to express them to the suffering and horror of the man who sits before him. How often do we bluster on about concerns that our hearers do not have? How often do we search for the eloquent word, the turn of phrase, rather than listen for the genuine concerns of those who have need of a specific and useful truth? Whenever we do the former, we are dupes and scoffers rather than mouthpieces of the living God.

And that leads us to the third of our dangerous words, and perhaps the one most common in the Hebrew text, namely the fool. The basic meanings of the noun *casil* are "fat," "dull," or "clumsy." The metaphorical

5. Holbert, *Preaching Job*, 11–13, 23–31.

meaning of the word occurs clearly in Jer 10:8 when he castigates idols, as opposed to the living YHWH, as "both stupid and foolish; the instruction given by idols is no better than wood!" Though the precise meaning of the last part of the Hebrew phrase, however delightfully scathing, is less than clear, the point remains clear enough: idols know nothing, unlike YHWH who, "among all the wise ones of the nations and in all their kingdoms," is unmatched in greatness and might (Jer 10:6–7). With YHWH there is wisdom; with idols there is only foolishness.

The accusations against foolishness take many forms. In Ps 49, a long poem against the dangers of wealth, fools are said to "boast in the abundance of their riches" (Ps 49:6), but in the end, they "cannot abide in their pomp; they are like the animals that perish. Such is the fate of the fool, the end of those who are comfortable in their lot" (Ps 49:12–13). Here fools are oblivious, satisfied, unaware of their need to be alert to life's challenges and changes. Prov 26 offers a long disquisition on the status of fools. As certain as "snows in winter" so is honor unfitting for fools (Prov 26:1); just as horses need whips and donkeys bridles, so do fools need a rod for their backs, since they are as recalcitrant and unyielding as horses and donkeys (Prov 26:3); fools must be corrected and challenged over and over, "lest they be wise in their own eyes" (Prov 26:5); it is the same idiocy to "cut off one's foot and to swallow violence" than "to send a message by the hand of a fool" (Prov 26:6); in the same way that the legs of a handicapped one hang limp, so does a proverb in the mouth of a fool (Prov 26:7). And on and on the poet goes, skewering the fool in as many ways as his fertile imagination can conjure. Fools are in constant need of correction, they cannot be trusted to bring a clear message to anyone, they forever imagine themselves to be wise, and they cannot give helpful advice, nor apparently cannot even tell a joke well!

The central theme for the fool appears to be her continual claim to be wise, when all discern that she is merely a fool who only imagines her wisdom (Prov 26:12), but in fact "hates knowledge" (Prov 1:22) or who actively "suppresses wisdom" (Prov 14:33). Another statement of this dangerous problem may be found at Prov 28:26: "Those who trust in their own wits are fools, but those who walk in wisdom come through safely." A fine proverbial summary of the question may be found at Eccl 4:13: "Better is a poor but wise youth than an old and foolish king, who will no longer take advice." Note the several insights of this proverb: poverty is no bad thing if it is accompanied by wisdom (wealth is far from a guarantee of wisdom);

power, too, is no guarantee of wisdom (aged kings can be foolish with all their power); the basic problem for this king is that he has ceased hearing any correction from anyone else.

It does not take a very wise person to see how preachers can become fools in this biblical sense. We too often claim a wisdom and a knowledge we do not have, expounding on subjects we in fact know very little about. I have a doctor of philosophy degree in the study of the Hebrew Bible, but that means only that I know something about one ancient document, or more specifically a few of the separate shorter documents contained within the larger document, along with some things about subjects related to that document. And that is all! My knowledge of politics, history, foreign languages, culture, economics, etc. is limited by what I am able to read and discern about those subjects, and is not based in a continuous and deep study of those complex areas of life. Too often I have expatiated long and loudly about those things that I knew less about than I wished to reveal. I could stand a huge dose of humility. What about you?

And that is where this brief study of three negative states in the book of Proverbs leads. We preachers are in desperate need of humility, an overriding conviction that we know less than we claim, and speak too often about subjects with which we are less than familiar. So, should we then simply shut up, cease our attempts to preach at all, and resort to a weekly worshipful hymn sing? I think not. Lady Wisdom would not have us silent, but wise. Wisdom for us is the recognition of our shortcomings as well as our strengths. If we are called to speak of subjects that are beyond our natural ken, and we very often are so called, wisdom bids us to be aware of what little we do know, and then demands that we study hard to become more alert to that subject.

A personal example may be helpful. Some years ago, I was called to serve a large congregation in a city near my own that had been riven with unmitigated disaster. The well-known and long-serving pastor of that church had been accused by several women of sexual improprieties, and he had summarily been removed from the leadership of the church. However, he refused to admit any wrongdoing, and many in the congregation who had loved him and followed his excellent leadership for many years also refused to believe such accusations about their pastor. I was asked to serve as interim minister. I knew very little about inappropriate sexual behaviors among clergy, but I set out very quickly to school myself in the subject. If I was to lead and to preach, I simply had to know far more than I did about such things. I heard the call of Lady Wisdom to me, and fortunately I heeded her call. By the time I ended my ministry there, I was hardly an expert in clergy sexual malfeasance. However, I had read enough, and listened carefully enough to those who had been abused, to speak of the subject with clarity and force. My own naiveté was conquered by a sense of humility that I was at first over my head and needed to find ways to come up to speed. How grateful I was, and still am, for those who helped me become more fully aware of the horrors that we humans can perpetrate on one another. I was, at the beginning of my time with that church, a genuine fool, a simpleton, and a dupe who could have easily fallen prey to the siren call of remaining each of those things. I did not, because God, through Lady Wisdom, called more loudly to follow the way of wisdom.

I write this small essay during another of my country's presidential contests, those every-four-years exercises that test the resolve of the candidates and the strained patience of the voters. In this 2016 cycle we seem cursed more than usual with dolts, simpletons, and fools! I do not use these harsh terms merely as cheapshots at those I do not like; they are in fact accurate designations of too many of those who would be president of my country. Their appalling lack of experience and knowledge, and their astonishing willingness to trumpet both as peculiar signs of greatness, make them the mountebanks that they are. Would that they could hear the cry of Lady Wisdom, shouted in the streets. Fools, give up your foolishness! Simpletons, how long will you love being simple! Dolts, how long will you allow others to tell you how to think and speak? Learn wisdom! Open your minds to her call! Preachers and politicians simply cannot allow themselves the unenviable luxury of lazy thoughts and sluggish and repetitious actions. Lady Wisdom calls to us! Will we not hear her call?

8

Born of Zion

Carolyn J. Sharp

This sermon was preached on 23 August 2017 during orientation for new students at Yale Divinity School in New Haven, Connecticut. The focal text was Ps 87; Rom 11:25–29 was also read.

Did you know that the memoirist, poet, and activist Maya Angelou was a singer and dancer when she first started out? In the fifties, Angelou sang calypso, and in the sixties, she sang the blues. Later she would sing through her poetry. And she danced! In wonderful candid photographs of Angelou taken in the early years of her career, even when she is hard at work on her writing, you can glimpse the dancer in her. In one early photo, she's flung herself onto her bed and is writing in longhand on a legal pad; books are strewn about her, but she is completely focused and centered. In another photo, she's propelled herself on to the floor, writing intently amidst newspapers and scattered playing cards. A third photo shows Angelou poised half off a bed, so focused on a magazine that it looks like she is diving off the bed into its pages. Angelou was so present to her work that she seemed heedless of her surroundings, flinging herself body and soul into whatever space she inhabited in *that* moment of creativity, *that* moment of truth-telling.[1]

Maya Angelou was born of giftedness and resolve. Now, she went through a lot. An African American girl growing up in Arkansas in the 1930s, she experienced outrageous moments of bigotry and violation. As a young child, she survived trauma so extreme that it rendered her mute for years. But she had been born of giftedness and resolve—so she listened and learned, and then she claimed her voice, telling her truth in every liminal space in which she found herself.[2]

Psalm 87 knows about that,
About claiming the truth of who we are
     even in liminal spaces,
       when we've left home and everything is unfamiliar,
       when we're scouting new terrain that feels like adventure,
         feels like the brightening of dawn,
         but also feels a little like being lost.
Psalm 87 is a song about community.
This ancient liturgical poem celebrates the repatriation of those
     who have *always* belonged to Zion,
     no matter what chains they have known,
     no matter what compromises they've had to make,
     no matter what they've left behind.

1. In a photo taken years later, Angelou is in the foreground and you can see her desk in the background: small and piled high with stacks of papers and photographs, it clearly was not a space for active working. When she traveled, Angelou's productive use of liminal space apparently extended to the practice of booking an extra hotel room just for writing. See Tanaka, "Inner Rooms of Maya Angelou."

2. Among the honors Maya Angelou received are dozens of honorary doctorates, three Grammy awards for spoken-word albums, the National Medal of Arts, and the Presidential Medal of Freedom. Perhaps her most famous work is the autobiographical *I Know Why the Caged Bird Sings* (1969), incorporated now into *The Collected Auto-biographies of Maya Angelou* (The Modern Library; New York: Random House, 2004). Among her best-loved poems are "On the Pulse of Morning," which she recited at the 1993 inauguration of Bill Clinton as President, and "Still I Rise," published in a poetry collection in 1978. Maya Angelou was Reynolds Professor of American Studies at Wake Forest University from 1982 until her death in 2014. In 2002, the Wake Forest School of Medicine founded the Maya Angelou Center for Health Equity, and in 2017, Wake Forest opened a new student residence hall named after Angelou.

"This one and that one" were born in Zion—
        were born *of Zion,* you understand[3]—
        born of holiness and grace and the joy of God drawing them home!

So: where are you from? Of what were you born?
What are the springs of creativity and struggle and difference
        that make you the *blessing* that you are?
What clarity or confusion, what crises and convictions
        have yielded you, here, among us today in this holy space?

Today you're not just "joining" the community here at YDS.
You belong here, and you're *creating* this community—
        which is full of singers and dancers, actual ones, yes . . .
        and also folks singing the gorgeous polyphony of theology,
        folks leaping joyfully into liturgy and ethics and church history,
        folks choreographing new steps in Latinx Christianity
        or singing the urgent cadences of Religion & Ecology.
We can't wait to see what you'll do here,
        the good work you'll accomplish,
        the beauty you'll offer, and the joy,
        and the fierce resistance to those things that aren't yet true enough.

It's time to sing to the LORD a new song,
        time to dance . . .
and sure, on the pragmatic side, it's time to tuck into more hours of reading
than you ever thought possible (*so many hours!*), and to spend days fighting
your way
        toward a new insight in that Intro to Theology paper.
It's time.
Whether you're sprawled across your bed at three in the morning,
        or sitting at the kitchen table after your toddlers go to sleep:
Stay present. Stay focused.

Figure out why you need a new interpretation of that Scripture passage.

3. The ancient poet is speaking metaphorically, as is clear from the trope of the Lord recording the names. Many of those deported from Judah in the first wave of deportations in 597 and older Judeans deported in 587 would not have lived to see the Persians' repatriation of Judean exiles in 538. This psalm was written for believers in the diaspora understood more broadly, possibly two centuries or more after the Babylonian exile.

Figure out why you love queer theory, and teach someone else about what you see there.
Figure out why you get so mad at Karl Barth.

And rejoice! Because whether it comes easy or hard, this is yours.
MDiv or MAR or STM,
just out of college or with undergrad twenty years back in the rearview mirror:
you were *born* for this holy place of curiosity and struggle and hard work.

Some of you come from Babylonia . . . others come from Tyre or Philistia. Let's be clear: I'm speaking metaphorically. There are no actual Philistines in the entering class that I know of, although I would like to say, some of your classmates and professors will be coming from a place you maybe don't love, from a set of theological commitments or liturgical practices that are utterly foreign to you. You may find *yourself* in exile in those moments when new learning unsettles you, when discernment is elusive or no one seems to get what's at stake for you in a discussion.

That's what this is. We sing and we dance *together,*
        in this community alive with fragility and contestation and joy.
God has brought you here for this liminal moment,
to fling yourself into hard work and sometimes not get enough sleep . . .
as you learn in pastoral care how wisdom about family systems and trauma theory can make all the difference when you respond to human brokenness,[4]
as you write your ethics paper dismantling the despicable distortions of white supremacy because you *know* God's justice will roll down like waters and righteousness like a permanent flash-flood[5];

---

4. Deepening one's pastoral wisdom and honing practical skills in pastoral care are essential for believers who understand compassion to lie at the core of authentic Christian theology. The psalmist's "All my springs are in you" may lead us to consider the troubled believer thirsting for God's presence (Ps 42); Ezekiel's vision of water flowing from the heavenly Temple, bringing life and healing to all it touches (Ezek 47); and Jesus's claim, "Those who drink of the water that I will give them will never be thirsty. The water that I give will become in them a spring of water gushing up to eternal life" (John 4:14). Medieval mystic and theologian Hildegard of Bingen addresses God with: "O Living Fountain, how great is Your sweet compassion!" in Book 3, Vision 13, paragraph 8 of her *Scivias* (Hildegard of Bingen, *Scivias,* 529).

5. "Permanent flash-flood": the phrase often translated "everflowing stream" in Amos 5:24 (נחלאיתן) is better understood as an everlasting flood of the sort that surges,

as you learn ways in which spiritual traditions throughout history have pointed to the One who is our peace.[6]

When it gets hard, remember Maya Angelou and *claim your voice.*
When you feel lost, remember Zion and *claim your home* in this liminal space.
And through it all, together we'll learn to bow before the Holy and whisper,
        "All my springs are in you."
Amen.

---

powerfully and with little warning, through dry streambeds in Palestine. Amos envisions not a charming brook but an unstoppable torrent of divine justice sweeping away all inequity.

6. "But now in Christ Jesus you who were once far off have been brought near by the blood of Christ. For he is our peace" (Eph 2:13–14). Israel longs for the Messiah as the Prince of Peace (Isa 9:7; see also Mic 5:5). Those who follow Jesus Christ can work in the confidence of his mighty power for justice and healing (Luke 4:16–21), as we seek to end our bitter divisions and stop the violence that for so long has disproportionately harmed women, LGBTQ folks, people of color, gender-nonconforming persons, and the poor.

9

God's Holy Place

Ps 24

Alma Tinoco Ruiz

I met my friend Daniel fifteen years ago. He was four years old. His parents Julia and Samuel are from México. Samuel played bass guitar in the praise group and frequently led Sunday worship services. Julia, who had suffered with lupus for many years, was a faithful member of the women's group. I was the pastor's wife and Daniel's Sunday school teacher. In fact, I was his Sunday school teacher for seven years. During those years, I made sure to teach him and the other kids all the biblical passages every kid should learn in Sunday school.

I taught them about the powerful God who separated the waters of the Red Sea, leading the Israelites to freedom from slavery.

I taught them about the God who gave young David the strength and courage to defeat the giant Goliath.

I taught them about the faithful God who saved Daniel from the lions.

I taught them about the servant God who was born in a manger.

I taught them about the merciful and compassionate God who gave sight to the blind, made the lame walk, made the deaf hear, cleansed people from leprosy, raised the dead, and proclaimed the good news to the poor and oppressed.

I taught them about God's love and sacrifice for all human beings.

And, of course, I taught them about the greatest commandment to love the Lord our God with all our heart, all our soul, all our mind, and all our strength, and to love our neighbors as ourselves.

And I also taught them that God is the creator of the earth and everything in it, and the one to whom it all belongs, as Ps 24 proclaims:

> The earth is the Lord's and all that is in it,
> the world, and those who live in it;
> for he has founded it on the seas,
> and established it on the rivers. (Ps 24:1–2)

We even painted a picture of the globe and wrote next to it: "The world belongs to the Lord and everything and all who lives in it." I remember telling my students that the trees, the birds, the flowers, the air we breathe, and everything we have belongs to the Lord. Daniel was the kind of kid who would ask: "So this pencil belongs to the Lord too?" He made me laugh as I answered, "Yes, but you get to take care of that pencil for God!"

When I left that church, I was very happy and proud of myself because I thought I had contributed, for seven wonderful years, to the Christian formation of Daniel and the other kids.

But, on Friday, November 23, 2018, nine years after I left that church, Daniel, his mom, and I were sitting on the carpet of my living room. Daniel, crying desperately, asked me: "Why did they take my dad away from me, Alma? He is a good Christian and a wonderful father. Why do they want to deport him to México? He loves God and he doesn't hurt anyone."

At that moment, I realized that I had failed Daniel and the other kids. I may have taught them wonderful stories about God, but I did not teach them the whole truth. I did not prepare them for the reality we experience in this fallen world. I enthusiastically taught them biblical stories where God triumphs over evil and where God heals, liberates, and transforms lives. I taught Daniel and the other kids the affirmation of Ps 24:1–2, but I neglected teaching them the reality of verses 3–6,

> 3 Who shall ascend the hill of the Lord?
> And who shall stand in his holy place?
> 4 Those who have clean hands and pure hearts,
> who do not lift up their souls to what is false,
> and do not swear deceitfully.

5 They will receive blessing from the Lord,
and vindication from the God of their salvation.
6 Such is the company of those who seek him,
who seek the face of the God of Jacob.

I painted for Daniel and the other kids a fruitful earth and a beautiful world that belongs to the Lord, an earth and a world as God has intended it to be: a world without borders, just as God's love for us; and a world in which humans can live in perfect communion with God, with God's creation, and with one another.

I failed to teach Daniel and the other kids that our journey to the holy place is difficult because even though God leads us through the Red Sea, some of us continue enslaving people for work, sex, pleasure, power, and money.

Our journey to the holy place is difficult because even though the Son of God has taught us to put away our arms, many of us insist in defeating with sling and stones all those who we consider our enemies.

Our journey to the holy place is difficult because even though God has showed us that he has the power to shut the mouths of the lions, most of us choose to bow down to the powers and principalities that threaten to send us to the lion's den.

Our journey to the holy place is difficult because even though we worship a servant and a humble God who became flesh in a manger, for some of us the main purpose in life is to achieve success, wealth, and power.

Our journey to the holy place is difficult because even though we proclaim that the Son of God was born and died for our salvation, many of us insist on "saving ourselves" by building walls and creating a false sense of national security.

Our journey to the holy place is difficult because even though we proclaim that our merciful and compassionate God is on the side of the sick, the poor, and the oppressed, most of us turn our backs to them.

Our journey to the holy place is difficult because God's greatest commandment has become just an option for many of us.

3 Who shall ascend the hill of the Lord?
And who shall stand in his holy place?
4 Those who have clean hands and pure hearts,
who do not lift up their souls to what is false,
and do not swear deceitfully.

5 They will receive blessing from the Lord,
and vindication from the God of their salvation.
6 Such is the company of those who seek him,
who seek the face of the God of Jacob.

I failed to teach my Sunday school students that most of us cannot come before the Lord with clean hands and pure hearts because our hands have been stained and our hearts have been contaminated by our worship of the idols of power and money.

I failed to teach them that there is a struggle between the powers of the devil and the power of God, a struggle that is presented in Luke 4:1–13 of Jesus' temptations. As Saint Romero affirms in one of his sermons, in each one of Jesus' temptations there are two plans: the plan of God and the plan of the devil.[1] The plan of the devil is a strategy of the gods of power and money to keep people captive, while the plan of God is to free people from the claws of evil.

> 1 Jesus, full of the Holy Spirit, returned from the Jordan and was led by the Spirit in the wilderness, 2 where for forty days he was tempted by the devil. He ate nothing at all during those days, and when they were over, he was famished. 3 The devil said to him, "If you are the Son of God, command this stone to become a loaf of bread." 4 Jesus answered him, "It is written, 'One does not live by bread alone.'"
> 5 Then the devil led him up and showed him in an instant all the kingdoms of the world. 6 And the devil said to him, "To you I will give their glory and all this authority; for it has been given over to me, and I give it to anyone I please. 7 If you, then, will worship me, it will all be yours." 8 Jesus answered him, "It is written,
> 'Worship the Lord your God,
> and serve only him.'"
> 9 Then the devil took him to Jerusalem, and placed him on the pinnacle of the temple, saying to him, "If you are the Son of God, throw yourself down from here, 10 for it is written,
> 'He will command his angels concerning you,
> to protect you,'
> 11 and 'On their hands they will bear you up,
> so that you will not dash your foot against a stone.'"
> 12 Jesus answered him, "It is said, 'Do not put the Lord your God to the test.'"

---

1. Romero, "Lent Is the Triumph of God's Saving Plan in History."

In Jesus' answers to the devil's temptations, we can witness in Jesus what Alyce M. McKenzie calls the four pillars of wisdom: living by loyalty to something or someone; living alert and alive to each moment of experience; living with self-discipline in our speech and actions; and living with the moral courage that empowers us to speak and act in accordance with our loyalties.[2] Even though Jesus was very hungry, he remained loyal to the Father to the end. Even though Jesus was very tired, he carefully listened to the devil's offers and cleverly refuted them with God's word. Even though Jesus was experiencing immediate physical needs, Jesus forwent short-term gratification for longer-term benefits.[3] Even though Jesus was physically weak, he had the courage to disrupt the devil's plans by exposing his evil intentions.

Many of us have foolishly fallen into the devil's traps and have succumbed to his temptations. In our effort to provide for our immediate needs or, as often happens, for our wants and desires, we have tried to dominate the land and control and exploit the fruits it provides. We have fought to be in the high place and obtain all the authority and splendor. We have tested God by acting as if we had sovereignty over our lives and all of God's creation.

> 3 Who shall ascend the hill of the Lord?
> And who shall stand in his holy place?
> 4 Those who have clean hands and pure hearts,
> who do not lift up their souls to what is false,
> and do not swear deceitfully.
> 5 They will receive blessing from the Lord,
> and vindication from the God of their salvation.
> 6 Such is the company of those who seek him,
> who seek the face of the God of Jacob.

Because humanity has fallen into the devil's temptations, our hearts and hands are stained. They are stained by the offerings we have brought before the gods of power and money. We have offered them the blood of the Native Americans. We have offered them the suffering of the African enslaved. We have offered them the lives of many innocent people who die in the wars we have initiated for power and wealth. We have offered them

2. McKenzie, *Hear and Be Wise*, xii.
3. McKenzie, *Hear and Be Wise*, 107.

the continual dehumanization of people of color and LGBTQ people. We have offered them the continual oppression of the poor and marginalized. We have offered them a huge wall that intends to divide the Lord's land. We have offered them children in cages and parents with a broken heart.

I did not know how to tell Daniel that his father's detention by ICE, his mother's devastation, and his own tears, were also an offering to the idols of power and money.

> 7 Lift up your heads, O gates!
> and be lifted up, O ancient doors!
> that the King of glory may come in.
> 8 Who is the King of glory?
> The Lord, strong and mighty,
> the Lord, mighty in battle.
> 9 Lift up your heads, O gates!
> and be lifted up, O ancient doors!
> that the King of glory may come in.
> 10 Who is this King of glory?
> The Lord of hosts,
> he is the King of glory. (Ps 24:7–10)

For the following couple of days, I could not look Daniel in the eyes. But on Tuesday, November 27, 2018, once Samuel, Daniel's father, was deported to México, we had a vigil outside the ICE detention center in Cary, North Carolina. It was a very cold night. I went up the platform we built to welcome and thank the people who joined us that night. My body was shivering, my face was frozen, I could barely utter a word. When I finally managed to say, "Thank you for being here," I looked at the people who were there, the women, the men, the youth, the kids, the Christians, the Jews, the ones who don't profess any religion. They were also shivering, their faces were also frozen, but they were there welcoming the King of glory in our midst. They were there that cold night in November, imploring the King of glory to come into the cell where Samuel was detained and to fill him with divine peace and love. They were there to ask the King of glory to come into the hearts of the government officials, the judges, the ICE officers, and all people who have something to do with the separation of families and clean their hearts and hands, as Jesus cleansed the body of the man with leprosy. They gathered that cold night to implore the Lord strong and mighty to destroy the walls and borders that separate Daniel from his father and many other kids and youth from their parents.

After witnessing how much these people care for Daniel, his family, and the many families who have been separated by unjust immigration laws, I was able to look Daniel in the eyes again and affirm to him that the powerful God that separated the waters of the Red Sea, the God who gave young David the strength and courage he needed, the faithful God who shut the mouths of the lions, the servant God who was born in a manger, the merciful and compassionate God who healed the sick, raised the dead, and comforted the poor and oppressed, is still working in our lives, cleansing our hands, and purifying our hearts, so that we may grow in our love for God and our neighbors, making it possible for us to love others beyond the borders and walls we have created.

May we all ascend to the mountain of the Lord and stand in God's holy place with clean hands and pure hearts. Amen.

10

"The Wisdom to Know the Difference"

Eccl 3:1–8; Jas 3:13–18

BEVERLY A. ZINK-SAWYER

IN THE SUMMER OF 2019, as we marked the 50th anniversary of the first landing on the moon, another anniversary of sorts occurred on that same day, but passed with little notice. July 20, 2019, was the 75th anniversary of the most serious attempt to assassinate Adolf Hitler and end his reign of terror. One of the individuals accused in that plot is a name familiar to those of us in the Reformed Protestant tradition and beyond: Dietrich Bonhoeffer. Bonhoeffer was a German Protestant pastor whose writings about theology and ethics and the practice of Christian discipleship continue to shape our faith today. His work as one of the founders of the Confessing Church, a group of Protestants who resisted the Nazi government's efforts to take over even the German churches, landed him in prison and then condemned him to death when he was associated with the conspirators of the July 20, 1944, attempt on Hitler's life. Scholars still debate when and even if Bonhoeffer actually turned from his strong pacifist convictions to participate in any organized efforts to assassinate Hitler, but all agree that he decided at some point that the time had come and the evil that was the Nazi regime had to be destroyed.

"For everything there is a season, and a time for every matter under heaven" (Eccl 3:1). Thus begins one of the most familiar passages of Scripture. Lines of this text have given themselves to authors and poets and, of course, composers—as many of us know from the Pete Seeger song made popular in the 1960s by The Byrds, "Turn, Turn, Turn." The text mentions "time" in every verse: a time to do this, and a time to do that. But it's not really about "time." Instead, this text is really about *discernment*: about knowing just *when* to do *what*. It's about what has been called "wisdom" through the ages.

Wisdom. It's one of the most ancient of human qualities and yet one of the most elusive. There's no doubt that it has loomed large throughout human history. Indeed, everybody from Socrates to Oprah has weighed in on the importance of wisdom. The Bible is full of references to it. There's even a whole genre of biblical literature devoted to wisdom: books like Proverbs, Ecclesiastes, and Song of Solomon. Jesus taught us to be "wise as serpents and innocent as doves." And the apostle Paul warned us that the wisdom we come to know in Christ may well appear as foolishness to the world. No, there's no shortage of wisdom about wisdom. But wisdom, like beauty, seems to be in the eye of the beholder. Defining "wisdom" is not unlike the Supreme Court's famous debate about pornography in the 1960s. In the midst of the deliberations over precisely what constituted pornographic material, Justice Potter Stewart admitted that he might not be able to define it. But he went on to say, "I know it when I see it."

The same could be said for wisdom. We might not be able to define it, but we know it when we see it. And see it we do: in so many people, and places, and ways. Think for a moment about the "wise" people who have shaped your life: parents, grandparents, teachers, pastors, neighbors, friends. I bet you could keep thinking all day about the people who gave you wise counsel in a moment of uncertainty; who spoke the right words when you needed to hear them; who encouraged and inspired you and showed you the way. And I bet most of those people—not all, but most— had some age on them. It's not an accident that we tend to associate wisdom with age. The grim reality of wisdom is that it only grows in the seedbed of pain. Or as that great wise man, Mark Twain, once said: "Good judgment is the result of experience, and experience [is] the result of bad judgment." In many cultures—Native, African, Asian—the elderly are revered for their wisdom, most often the elderly *women*, the matriarchs of the society.

They've navigated the shoals of life and landed safely on a better shore. And now they help others make their way through the waters.

What is wisdom? Where does it come from? How do we get it? These questions are as old as thinking humans, and their answers remain elusive. There's even a branch of neuroscience that studies wisdom to see if it reveals any neural pathways that can be identified and duplicated. Maybe the reason wisdom is so hard to define is because it isn't a *thing*, but an approach, an inclination, a mindset. Wisdom isn't a body of knowledge or a set of facts. It's a leaning of the *heart* as well as the *mind:* the kind of leaning that prompted an ardent pacifist like Dietrich Bonhoeffer to risk—and *lose*—his life when he felt the time had come to resist evil. Wisdom is the kind of leaning that comes from hard-won experience and from *listening*—careful listening—to the voices of others and, especially, to the voice of God. That's the "wisdom from above" that James in his New Testament letter challenges us as Christian disciples to seek. It's clear from James's portrait of the wise person that wisdom is not about *what you know,* but *how you live.* Wisdom reveals itself in gentleness and mercy, in goodness and peace. It rejects selfish ambition, hypocrisy, and boastfulness. It abhors what is "false to the truth." Hmmm, sounds like some qualities that are in short supply these days.

"For everything there is a season, and a time for every matter under heaven" (Eccl 3:1). "Who is wise and understanding among you? Show by your good life that your works are done with gentleness born of wisdom" (James 3:13). What the world needs now is wisdom, discernment: the ability to know when to speak out for justice, and when to work quietly for change; when to build bridges, and when to dismantle walls; when to hold ourselves and each other accountable, and when to extend mercy and grace. The truth is, we'll never know exactly what time it is; we'll never have the perfect wisdom that always gets things right. But we keep on keeping on, using all the gifts God has given us: loving hearts and thinking minds, communities of faith and conversation, gifts of grace in the form of word and sacrament, and, most comforting of all, the assurance of forgiveness even when we get it wrong.

There's a prayer that we all are familiar with, the original version of which is attributed to American theologian Reinhold Niebuhr. The version we know is called the Serenity Prayer. It captures well the sense of direction, the wisdom for living that can only come from communion with God. The prayer implores God for peace in our moments of frustration with the way things are and asks for courage when we see a way that we can act to make things better. But the most important line of the prayer is the last one, seeking wisdom—discernment—to judge between the two:

God grant me the serenity to accept the things I cannot change,

Courage to change the things I can,

And the wisdom to know the difference.

May it be so. Amen.

11

"Embodying Wisdom Under Imperial Duress"

Luke 2:41–52

ÁNGEL J. GALLARDO, PHD

SECTION I. INTRODUCTION

THE CHRISTIAN FAITH REVOLVES around the scandalous claim that Jesus of Nazareth is God incarnate. As John's Gospel puts it, "the Word of God became flesh and dwelt among us" (John 1:14 KJV). This radical conviction led early Christians to see Jesus as the Messiah, the one who fulfills Israel's covenant. By extension, that proclamation means that Jesus embodied Israel's wisdom tradition—a reality conveyed by the gospel writers. "Jesus is both teacher of wisdom and Wisdom in Person."[1] As Alyce McKenzie notes, "Matthew's goal is for readers to acknowledge Jesus as the God-authorized interpreter of tradition (Wisdom of God) and to live by his teachings."[2] In other words, Jesus is wisdom made flesh.

To a certain extent, every Gospel portrays Jesus as a sage. The Gospel of Luke, however, is the only one that provides a glimpse of *how* Jesus "increased in wisdom" (Luke 2:52). Luke relays two stories that describe

1. McKenzie, *Preaching Biblical Wisdom in a Self-Help Society*, 179.
2. McKenzie, *Preaching Biblical Wisdom in a Self-Help Society*, 179.

a process of maturation. In the first story, Mary and Joseph travel to the temple in Jerusalem, where they encounter Anna and Simeon, to dedicate infant Jesus in accordance with Mosaic law (Luke 2:22–40). The first story ends with the phrase: "the child grew and became strong, filled with wisdom; and the favor of God was upon him" (Luke 2:40 DBH).

However, I want to focus on the second story because today is Higher Education Sunday, a day in which we recognize recent graduates and celebrate their accomplishments.[3] In the second story, Luke recounts an episode in which a twelve-year-old Jesus abandons his parents in order to remain in Jerusalem. If you think about it, this is the only biblical text that describes what Jesus was like as a pre-teen, as a young man. This story deserves our attention because it reveals the maturation Jesus undergoes in order to fully embody the Wisdom of God. By carefully examining this passage, I hope to highlight some practical lessons for those of us, and especially our recent graduates, who seek to follow the "crucified and risen sage."[4]

SECTION II

Our story begins with Mary, Joseph, and Jesus traveling to Jerusalem. According to Luke, this journey occurred every year, which was no small feat because Jerusalem is approximately sixty-four miles from Nazareth. With the passage of time, Mary and Joseph would embark on an arduous journey with an infant, a small child, and eventually a young boy. Anyone who has traveled with children can attest how challenging a long road trip can be. It is truly a spiritual test.

I learned this lesson on a flight several years ago. Although I grew up in Los Angeles, I spent many summers with family in Mexico City. And on one of those flights, I recall sitting next to Lucy, a young mother of modest means, and her two-year old son, Miguel. Lucy was dressed to impress. Her make-up was on point, she wore a matching outfit, and sported a fancy hair style. But all this would change after take-off. During the flight, Miguel screamed, cried, kicked the seats, and, of course, he soiled his diaper. No one got any rest. Lucy apologized numerous times to the other passengers. Prior to landing, Miguel fell asleep; he knocked out. Lucy, on the other hand, appeared exhausted. Her hair was out of place, her mascara was

3. A version of this sermon was preached at St. Luke "Community" United Methodist Church Higher Education Sunday.

4. McKenzie, *Preaching Biblical Wisdom in a Self-Help Society*, xxii.

smeared, her clothes were dirty, and her personal belongings were scattered on the floor.

But before parting ways, I asked Lucy, "What brings you to Mexico?" I will never forget her response. She said, "Well, the truth is, I was undocumented for a long time. This meant I could not leave the US without the risk of being permanently separated from my husband and children. As a result, I didn't see my parents for nearly fifteen years. However, since I recently became a Permanent Resident, I decided to introduce my son to his grandparents in Mexico City. I want him to know where we came from." And then it hit me. This mother went through all that trouble to connect her son with his heritage, to connect him to his people.

According to Luke, Mary and Joseph did something similar. You see, every spring, Mary and Joseph would pack their bags and with the little money they had saved up they embarked on a long and dangerous journey. As twenty-first-century readers, you might wonder, "Why go through all that trouble? Couldn't they just worship God from the comfort of Nazareth?" The truth is that Mary and Joseph embarked on this journey out of obedience. They traveled to Jerusalem every year with a single purpose: to celebrate the Passover. Like so many Jews throughout the centuries, Jesus' family went to great lengths to remember how Yahweh liberated them from slavery in Egypt. This yearly ritual was part of the way in which elders passed on the wisdom tradition to the next generation. As a boy, and eventually as a young man, Jesus grew up hearing stories about Yahweh's solidarity. One could reasonably conclude that such exposure taught him *how* to embody God's preferential option for the poor and the oppressed.

SECTION III

Luke tells us that when the Passover ended, Mary and Joseph began their return to Galilee. But unbeknownst to them, Jesus stayed behind. It wasn't until the next day that they noticed his absence. Now, you may be wondering, "How could they lose track of him for an entire day?" While it may seem that Mary and Joseph were irresponsible parents, keep in mind that they were traveling in a large caravan with other Galileans. Mary and Joseph trusted their people to keep him safe.

This attitude is not uncommon today. When I was in middle school, I could play in the church parking lot for hours without my parents batting an eye because they trusted the older kids to care for the younger ones.

They knew that if I acted up, other adults would set me straight. As long I was with our spiritual kin, my parents knew I would be alright. Likewise, Mary and Joseph trusted their community. They knew that their fellow Galileans would look out for their boy. But eventually they began asking, "Have you seen Jesus? Have you seen our son?"

In order to grasp this question's significance, we must hear it within its historical context. We must remember that at the time, Israel suffered under Roman occupation, which subordinated Jews in their own land. While Rome claimed to be a regime of law and order, the reality on the ground was quite different. We know how empires treat colonial subjects. Throughout history, empires have used psychological warfare, economic pressure, and sexual or physical violence to enforce the status quo. Like many communities of color today, first-century Jews lived under the constant threat of state-sanctioned violence. We must never forget that Jesus lived his entire life under such conditions.

These social realities should help shed light on Mary and Joseph's concerns. Can you imagine what they were thinking? As any concerned mother, Mary was probably asking, "What if he got separated from the group? What if he got lost and ran into some Roman soldiers? Joseph, we have to do something; our boy might be in danger!" Fear likely filled them with anxiety. Such concerns were not unreasonable. In the end, the Romans would hang their son from a cross.

SECTION IV

Let's consider what happens when Mary and Joseph finally reunite with Jesus.

According to Luke, after retracing their steps back to the capital city, they found Jesus at the temple sitting with the doctors of the law, listening and asking questions. He stayed behind in order to study with the sages of his day. These scholars spent decades analyzing the Scriptures, reciting the Psalms, and debating ancient prophecies. Apparently, "all who heard him were amazed at his understanding and his answers." The fact that Jesus was giving answers suggests the doctors were asking questions. In other words, the religious elders were interested in hearing what a soon-to-be-teenager had to say. This insight made me wonder whether the church is truly learning from the youth. Are bishops, pastors, and theological educators listening to the needs, interests, and concerns of younger generations? Our youth might be wiser than we think; the question is whether we are wise enough to listen.

Notice that before ever becoming a rabbi (teacher), Jesus had to undergo a process of transformation. Luke alludes to this process in verse 52 by writing that Jesus "increased in wisdom and in stature and in favor with God and man." Before delivering the Sermon on the Mount, Jesus had to learn, to develop, to grow. Biblical scholars have translated the phrase "increased in stature" as "coming into maturity." Like the rest of humankind, Jesus had to *become* wise.[5] This point might sound controversial to some.

You might be wondering, "But if God is all-knowing, and Jesus had to learn, then how could he be God? How could Jesus increase in wisdom yet still be divine?" While such questions sound reasonable, they depart from the wrong place. They ultimately misunderstand the way in which we come to know God. As theologian Willie Jennings points out, Jesus "learns the wisdom of his people—their way with the earth, with the land, with animals . . . he works with his hands and he works the land. This crucial reality . . . has always been difficult for Christians to remember because we have turned the idea of an all-knowing God against the God we know in Jesus. God does know—and in Jesus, God has chosen to learn with us."[6] At the heart of the incarnation is the idea that God shares in the form of the creature. So rather than starting with our preconceived notions about what divinity should look like, our theology of God should begin with the God revealed in Jesus of Nazareth, who is after all, wisdom made flesh.

SECTION V

I want to conclude by examining the interaction between Jesus and his earthly parents. According to Luke, Mary and Joseph were "astonished" to find him there. The text does not explain why Jesus failed to communicate his plans to remain in Jerusalem. Perhaps like pre-teens and teenagers of every generation, he thought he knew better. Maybe he thought, "I'm old enough to make my own decisions. I don't need to ask for permission. Besides, it's not like I'm doing anything wrong." After all, he was in the house of God.

I imagine they felt frustrated and upset. In fact, Mary asks, "Son, why have you treated us so? Your father and I have been searching for you in

5. See entry for *helikos* in Bauer, *Greek-English Lexicon of the New Testament,* 345.

6. Jennings, "Overcoming Racial Faith," 9.

great distress" (v. 48). After careful analysis of the original Greek, I developed a better translation: "Boy, how could you do that . . . do you know the hell you put us through?!" And, like a typical adolescent, Jesus seemed to have a bit of an attitude. He replies, "Why were you looking for me? Did you not know I would be in my Father's house?" In essence, Jesus says, "Mom, why are you trippin'? If you're stressed out, that is your fault. And, why do I need to listen to Joseph? He's not my real dad." If I had talked to my parents like this, I don't know if I would have lived to tell the story.

But let's not miss the valuable lesson in Jesus' actions. By choosing to be in his "Father's house" rather than returning to their home in Galilee, Jesus poses a stark contrast between his heavenly Father and his earthly parents. In doing so, he reminds Mary and Joseph of a harsh truth: God's will is more important than yours. Furthermore, Jesus reminds his parents—and by extension all earthly parents—that children ultimately belong to God, the Creator of heaven and earth. Earthly parents, whether adoptive or biological, are simply called by God to be wise and faithful stewards.

It might be difficult for parents or elders to hear this lesson, especially on Higher Education Sunday. Perhaps you want your daughter or son, granddaughter or grandson, mentee or nephew to pursue a certain career. Perhaps you have a belief system you want them to adopt or a lifestyle you want them to reject. But rather than telling our young people exactly what to do, we should equip them to pursue God's justice and peace in the world. We should empower them to follow the Spirit wherever it leads, even if that means going in a direction we did not anticipate. Above all else, our strongest means of persuasion should be our example.

I want to conclude by offering a final lesson to the youth, especially our junior high and high school graduates. Luke ends this story by writing: "And he went down with them and came to Nazareth and was submissive to them" (v. 52). You heard rightly. Jesus, the eternal Word of God, chose to submit to his earthly parents. While it might appear to be a sign of weakness, submission, in this context, is actually a marker of wisdom. It signifies maturity.

Listen up, young people. You might find the boundaries set by your parents to be unfair. You might find a curfew unnecessary. You might be annoyed when your parents call when you're out with your friends. You might be thinking, "I can take care of myself. Besides, nothing bad is going to happen." But keep in mind that God has entrusted your parents and extended family with your well-being. Remember that healthy boundaries are not meant to stifle; they are meant to help you thrive. Therefore, embodying wisdom entails taking ownership of your well-being. It means being prudent in all things. It means being wise about the entertainment and food you consume, with whom you spend time, who you date, which desires to indulge, and what professional ambitions to pursue. Because, after all, as disciples we are called to glorify God in all things.

SECTION VI. CONCLUSION

Graduates, I am here to tell you that Christian discipleship may require you to make hard decisions. You may have to choose between what the world expects from you and what God desires for you. You may be at a crossroads, asking yourself, "Should I continue down this path of convenience or pursue what God desires for me, even if it hurts?"

If you are scared or doubtful, rest assured you are in good company because Jesus himself faced inner turmoil. Recall his prayer in the garden of Gethsemane: "Father, if you are willing, remove this cup from me; yet, not my will but yours be done" (Luke 22:42). Nevertheless, because the Word became flesh, we can be confident that God understands our human condition. In Christ, God has faced our fears and overcome our temptations. God has even conquered death. And ultimately through Christ we too can be victorious!

12

Wisdom and Social Media

Nancy Kasten

In the documentary *The Social Dilemma* (Netflix, 2020), filmmaker Jeff Orlowski describes how artificial intelligence enables social media to manipulate human nature for corporate gain, to the detriment of mental health, democracy, and the planet. Through the film's interviews with original creators and promoters of social media, we come to understand that while this powerful technology was intended to be used as a force for good, its unintended consequences are eroding the well-being of individuals, families, and societies.

We don't need to watch a documentary to know that social media has changed our world. We thought the danger of a Facebook account was that we would sign up to find one former college roommate and end up with hundreds of "friends" who would distract us and waste our time. We never imagined that we would inadvertently advance a culture of polarization and extremism.

Users who turn to social media for information, entertainment, and commerce end up experiencing the anxiety, helplessness, despair, and isolation that lead to destructive behavior towards ourselves and others. Yet we remain addicted to our devices, continuing to expose ourselves to whatever might pop up on our screens. I challenge anyone to put their phone in one of the locked safes originally designed to help dieters delay their craving for cookies for an hour or two. It will make giving up cookies seem like a breeze. While the film warns of the dangers of a late twentieth-century innovation, the wakeup call it sounds is ancient:

> Wisdom cries aloud in the streets,
> Raises her voice in the squares.
> At the head of the busy streets she calls;
> At the entrance of the gates, in the city, she speaks out:
> How long will you simple ones love simplicity,
> You scorners be eager to scorn,
> You know-it-alls hate knowledge? . . .
> The tranquility of the simple will kill them,
> And the complacency of the arrogant will destroy them.
> (Prov 1:20–22, 32[1])

The documentary features professionals from the industry who are working to make technology more humane. But toothpaste can never go back in the tube. The tools have been created, and threats unleashed can never be sufficiently regulated or programmed away. We long to keep things simple, and artificial intelligence entices us with the simplicity of binary thinking. The text from Proverbs implores us to shed the complacency and hubris that keeps us funneling information into limited categories of black and white. As it suggests, our salvation depends on employing the rainbow spectrum of intelligence—the knowledge and wisdom that are granted to us by virtue of being created in God's image—to assert our humaneness and our humanity. Technology may be necessary to release us from the influence of social media, but it will never be sufficient.

Over and over again throughout human history we employ the tools we have at hand in the most expedient and self-serving fashion without pausing to ask ourselves what outcomes our behaviors might lead to. Artificial intelligence brilliantly commodifies this aspect of human nature. It starts with the conclusion, the goal, and then sets up a string of binary choices that will lead to that outcome. Simple. Artificial intelligence is not concerned with collateral damage caused along the way. Our evolution from animals programmed to instinctually fight, flee, or freeze in the face of perceived threats makes us prey to binary thinking, a weakness that social media exploits. But we are also created in God's image, able to overcome our instincts and weaknesses if we choose to. Our humanity depends

---

1. Editor's note: the translations in this sermon derive primarily from the Jewish Publication Society version Tanak, with some modifications from Rabbi Kasten.

on our ability to respond to pain and suffering with something other than competition, avoidance, or paralysis. Wisdom reminds us that we have additional resources: learning, discernment, understanding, recognition, awareness, insight, and perception, enabling us to make every choice in context, in the moment, with intention. This kind of intelligence cannot guarantee a product or outcome, but it does prevent us from putting on our blinders and chasing after vain pursuits—wealth, power, immortality: behavior that exacerbates the very pain and suffering we are desperately trying to avoid.

It seems impossible to go back to the beginning and start all over again. But that is what we are required to do. In an election prayer in 2016, Sikh activist and lawyer Valerie Kaur addressed our hopelessness and despair by asking, "What if this darkness is not the darkness of the tomb, but the darkness of the womb?"[2] We are not destined for either of these options. Every morning, Jewish prayer reasserts that in goodness God renews the works of creation every day for eternity. So, let's go back to the beginning and reimagine the world as it could be.

"The two of them were *arumim* (naked,) the human and his woman, and they were not ashamed. The serpent was the most *arum* (shrewdest) of all the land animals that the Lord God had made, and he said to the woman, 'Did God really say: you shall not eat of any tree of the garden?' The woman replied to the serpent, 'We may eat of the trees of the garden, but it is the fruit of the tree that is inside the garden that God told us we should not eat from it or touch it, lest we die.' The serpent said to the woman, 'You will not die, but God knows that when you eat from it your eyes will be opened and you will be like divine beings, knowing good and evil'" (Gen 3:1–5).

The narrative illuminates an irrefutable truth: human suffering is a consequence of human awakening. But the use of the same word, *arum*, to describe both nakedness and cunning also provides an oft-neglected antidote. The serpent, who is both naked and cunning, is the bridge between our animal nature and our human nature. While traditional exegesis has cast the serpent as a villain, the evil seducer who leads humanity to sin, in various ancient cultures it was a symbol of wisdom. In Eden, the serpent awakens humans to the unique attributes we inherit from our Divine progenitor.

> It is Wisdom calling
> Understanding raising her voice

2. Kaur, "Sikh Prayer for America," para. 3.

She takes her stand at the topmost heights
By the wayside, at the crossroads
Near the gates, at the city entrance; at the entryways she shouts:
"I call to men, but my cry is to all people-
Simple ones, learn Prudence (*Ormah*);
Arrogant ones, instruct your hearts." (Prov 8:1–5)

The Hebrew word for Prudence is *Ormah*, from the same root as *arum*. The serpent is naked and shrewd and prudent. Understanding human nature, it shrewdly ignites the woman's curiosity and opens a door to awareness of a reality in which good and evil are not binary choices but possibilities that coexist, qualities we can enhance or discourage. When they open their eyes, the woman and her man see that they are naked like animals, but they also have great power, like God. And borrowing a theme from another film, *Spider-Man*,[3] with great privilege comes great responsibility.

We will destroy ourselves if we see ourselves in the darkness of the tomb, outsourcing our decision-making to artificial intelligence, making binary choices, and applying our human intelligence only to making technology more humane. If this is to be the darkness of the womb, we must reclaim our human capacity for nonbinary decision making. We can embrace the opening of our eyes rather than resenting it, so that our nakedness can teach us to confront reality as it is, which is not either/or, but rich and complicated and challenging. In the words of the poet Joy Harjo, "Let's not shame our eyes for seeing. Instead, thank them for their bravery."[4]

Humans might be programmed to blame or complain, but we can choose to explain. Instead of leaving the explaining to God, or a king, or a president, or a supreme court justice, or a tech genius, we can access our own God-given gifts of knowledge, wisdom, and discernment. The trees in the garden are the tools which anyone can access for any purpose. The fruit of the tree of knowledge is the instruction manual that helps us understand the power those tools give us, for good or for evil.

Marianne Williamson writes,

Our deepest fear is not that we are inadequate.
Our deepest fear is that we are powerful beyond measure.

3. Raimi, *Spider-Man*.
4. Harjo, *Conflict Resolution for Holy Beings*, 39.

> It is our light, not our darkness
> That most frightens us.[5]

We need not fear technology if we are brave enough to recreate the world around it with knowledge, wisdom, discernment, and insight. We need not let fear determine our future. We have plenty of descriptions of a world created through blindness to suffering and rejection of knowledge. But Prov 8 gives us a deeper assurance—of wisdom woven into the first fabric of creation itself:

> God created Me before doing anything at all
> Before anything that was recorded,
> I was programmed in you before anything else,
> Understood before land and nation
> There was no "surface of the deep" when I was born. (Prov 8:22–24)

Wisdom, in the biblical tradition, is ancient and ever new. Present from the beginning, and still pointing us towards new possibilities, with all of the inevitable complexity and suffering that choice requires. We can only birth a new world of equity, loving-kindness, and hope if we are *arum*: present to new ideas, prudent in how we vet them, vigilant in our resistance to binary thinking, and open in compassion to the diversity of human experience in God's ongoing work of creation.

5. Williamson, *Return to Love.*

Bibliography

Allen, O. Wesley. *The Homiletic of All Believers: A Conversational Approach*. Louisville: Westminster John Knox, 2005.

———. *Preaching and the Human Condition*. Nashville: Abingdon, 2016.

Allen, Ronald. *Preaching the Topical Sermon*. Louisville: Westminster John Knox, 1992.

Allen, Ronald J., et al. *Theology for Preaching: Authority, Truth and Knowledge of God in a Postmodern Ethos*. Nashville: Abingdon, 1997.

Alter, Robert. *The Book of Psalms*. New York: Norton, 2007.

———. *The Wisdom Books*. New York: Norton, 2010.

Avila, Rafael. *Worship and Politics*. Maryknoll, NY: Orbis, 1981.

Barton, Stephen C. "Gospel Wisdom." In *Where Shall Wisdom Be Found?: Wisdom in the Bible, the Church and the Contemporary World*, edited by Stephen C. Barton, 93–110. Edinburgh: T. & T. Clark, 1999.

———, ed. *Where Shall Wisdom Be Found?: Wisdom in the Bible, the Church and the Contemporary World*. Edinburgh: T. & T. Clark, 1999.

Bass, Dorothy C., et al. *Christian Practical Wisdom: What It Is, Why It Matters*. Grand Rapids, MI: Eerdmans, 2016.

Bauer, Walter, et al., eds. *A Greek-English Lexicon of the New Testament and Other Early Christian Literature*. Chicago: University of Chicago Press, 1979.

Beard, Mary. *Women and Power: A Manifesto*. New York: Norton, 2017.

Bieler, Andrea, and Hans-Martin Gutmann. *Embodying Grace: Proclaiming Justification in the Real World*. Translated by Linda M. Maloney. Minneapolis: Fortress, 2010.

Bland, Dave. *Proverbs and the Formation of Character*. Eugene, OR: Cascade, 2015.

Blount, Brian K. *Go Preach! Mark's Kingdom Message and the Black Church Today*. Maryknoll, NY: Orbis, 1998.

Botterweck, G. Johannes, Helmer Ringgren, and Heinz-Josef Fabry, eds. *Theological Dictionary of the Old Testament*. Vol. 12. Translated by Douglas W. Stott. Grand Rapids: Eerdmans, 2012.

Bowlin, John. "Proclaiming the Gospel, Preaching the Public." *Theology Today* 70.1 (April 2013) 9–15.

Brown, Sally. "Discerning the Public Presence of God." *Theology Today* 70.1 (April 2013) 30–37.

Buttrick, David. *Homiletic: Moves and Structures*. Minneapolis: Fortress, 1987.

———. *Jesus Christ: An Exercise in Homiletic Theology*. Minneapolis: Fortress, 1988.

———. *Preaching the New and the Now*. Louisville: Westminster John Knox, 1998.

Cahalan, Kathleen A. "Spiritual Practices and the Search for a Wisdom Epistemology." In *Christian Practical Wisdom: What It Is, Why It Matters*, edited by Dorothy C. Bass et al., 275–321. Grand Rapids: Eerdmans, 2016.

Camp, Claudia V. *Wisdom and the Feminine in the Book of Proverbs*. Columbia, GA: Almond, 1985.

Campbell, Charles L. *Preaching Jesus: The New Directions for Homiletics in Hans Frei's Postliberal Theology*. Grand Rapids, MI: Eerdmans, 1997. Reprint, Eugene, OR: Wipf & Stock, 2016.

———. *Word Before the Powers: An Ethic of Preaching*. Louisville: Westminster John Knox, 2002.

Clifford, Richard J. "Introduction to Wisdom Literature." In *The New Interpreter's Bible*, edited by Leander E. Keck, 5:1–16. Nashville: Abingdon, 1997.

———. *Proverbs: A Commentary*. Old Testament Library. Louisville: Westminster John Knox, 1999.

Cone, James. *The Cross and the Lynching Tree*. Maryknoll, NY: Orbis, 2011.

Crenshaw, James L. *Ecclesiastes*. The Old Testament Library. Louisville: Westminster John Knox, 1987.

Davis, Ellen F. "The Preacher as Public Imaginer." E. J. Prevatte Biblical Lectures, Campbell University, November 6, 2018.

———. *Proverbs, Ecclesiastes, and the Song of Songs*. Louisville: Westminster John Knox Press, 2000.

Deane-Drummond, Celia. *Creation Through Wisdom: Theology and the New Biology*. Edinburgh: T. & T. Clark, 2000.

———. *The Wisdom of the Liminal: Evolution and Other Animals in Human Becoming*. Grand Rapids: Eerdmans, 2014.

Diugan, John, dir. *Romero*. Burbank, CA: Warner Bros. Pictures, 1989.

"Do Politics Belong in Church? 11 Pastors and Theologians Weigh in." *The Christian Century*, September 24, 2018. https://www.christiancentury.org/article/opinion/do-politics-belong-church

Dodd, Charles Harold. *The Apostolic Preaching and Its Development*. New York: Harperand Bros., 1944. Reprint, Grand Rapids, MI: Baker, 1980.

Draper, Paul, and Ryan Nichols. "Diagnosing Bias in Philosophy of Religion." *The Monist* 96 (2013) 420–46.

Dubois, W. E. B. *The Souls of Black Folks*. New York: Penguin, 1969.

Dunn, James D. G. "Jesus: Teacher of Wisdom or Wisdom Incarnate?" In *Where Shall Wisdom Be Found?: Wisdom in the Bible, the Church and the Contemporary World*, edited by Stephen C. Barton, 75–92. Edinburgh: T. & T. Clark, 1999.

Farley, Edward. *Practicing Gospel: Unconventional Thoughts on the Church's Ministry*. Louisville: Westminster John Knox, 2003.ˆ

Foerde, Gerhard. *On Being a Theologian of the Cross: Reflections on Luther's Heidelberg Disputation, 1518*. Grand Rapids: Eerdmans, 1997.

———. *Theology Is for Proclamation*. Minneapolis: Augsburg Fortress, 1990.

Funkhouser, Eric. "Willing Belief and the Norm of Truth." *Philosophical Studies* 115 (2003) 179–95.

Gottwald, Norman K. *The Hebrew Bible: A Socio-Literary Introduction*. Philadelphia: Fortress, 1985.

Gross, Nancy Lammers. *Women's Voices and the Practice of Preaching*. Grand Rapids: Eerdmans, 2017.

Hall, Douglas John. *The Cross in Our Context: Jesus and the Suffering World*. Minneapolis: Fortress, 2003.

Hardy, Daniel W. "The Grace of God and Earthly Wisdom." In *Where Shall Wisdom Be Found?: Wisdom in the Bible, the Church and the Contemporary World*, edited by Stephen C. Barton, 231–48. Edinburgh: T. & T. Clark, 1999.

Harjo, Joy. *Conflict Resolution for Holy Beings*. New York: Norton, 2017.

Hays, Richard B. "Wisdom According to Paul." In *Where Shall Wisdom Be Found?: Wisdom in the Bible, the Church and the Contemporary World*, edited by Stephen C. Barton, 111–24. Edinburgh: T. & T. Clark, 1999.

Heath, Brad, et al. "How a Lie Took Hold and Took Off." *The Courier Journal*, Thursday, November 1, 2018, B1–2.

Hendricks, Obery. *The Politics of Jesus: Rediscovering the True Revolutionary Nature of Jesus' Teachings and How They Have Been Corrupted*. Los Angeles: Three Leaves, 2007.

Hildegard of Bingen. *Scivias*. The Classics of Western Spirituality. New York: Paulist, 1990.

Holbert, John C. *Preaching Job*. Eugene, OR: Wipf & Stock, 1999.

Holbert, John C., and Alyce M. McKenzie. *What Not to Say*. Louisville: Westminster John Knox, 2011.

Jacobsen, David Schnasa. "Going Public with the Means of Grace: A Homiletical Theology of Promise for Word and Sacrament in a Post-secular Age." *Theology Today* 75 (2018) 371–82.

———. *Mark*. Fortress Biblical Preaching Commentaries. Minneapolis: Fortress, 2014.

———. "Preaching as the Unfinished Task of Theology: Grief, Trauma, and Early Christian Texts in Homiletical Interpretation." *Theology Today* 70 (2014) 407–16.

Jacobsen, David Schnasa, and Robert Kelly. *Kairos Preaching: Speaking Gospel to the Situation*. Minneapolis: Fortress, 2009.

Jennings, Willie James. "Overcoming Racial Faith." *Divinity* 14 (2015) 4–9.

———. "Speaking Gospel in the Public Arena." In *Preaching Gospel: Essays in Honor of Richard Lischer*, edited by Charles L. Campbell et al., 187–97. Lloyd John Ogilvie Institute of Preaching Series. Eugene, OR: Cascade, 2016.

Jeter, Joseph, Jr. *Crisis Preaching: Personal and Public*. Nashville: Abingdon, 1998.

Jones, Serene. *Trauma and Grace: Theology in a Ruptured World*. Louisville: Westminster John Knox, 2009.

Kaur, Valerie. "A Sikh Prayer for America." https://valariekaur.com/2016/11/a-sikh-prayer-for-america-on-november-9th-2016/.

Keohane, Joe. "How Facts Backfire: Researchers Discover a Surprising Threat to Our Democracy: Our Brains." *The Boston Globe*, July 14, 2010. http://archive.boston.com/news/science/articles/2010/07/11/how_facts_backfire/.

Kim, Eunjoo Mary. *Christian Preaching and Worship in Multicultural Contexts*. Collegeville, MN: Liturgical, 2017.

———. *Preaching the Presence of God: A Homiletic from an Asian American Perspective*. Valley Forge, PA: Judson, 1999.

King, Martin Luther, Jr. "Letter from a Birmingham Jail." https://www.africa.upenn.edu/Articles_Gen/Letter_Birmingham.html.

Klayman, Joshua. "Varieties of Confirmation Bias." *The Psychology of Learning and Motivation* 32 (1995) 385–418.

Kolbert, Elizabeth. "Why Facts Don't Change Our Minds: New Discoveries about the Human Mind Show the Limitations of Reason." *The New Yorker*, February 27, 2017. https://www.newyorker.com/magazine/2017/02/27/why-facts-dont-change-our-minds.

Lakeland, Paul. *Postmodernity: Christian Identity in a Fragmented Age*. Guides to Theological Inquiry. Minneapolis: Fortress, 1997.

Linklater, Kristin. *Freeing the Natural Voice*. Revised and expanded edition. Hollywood: Drama, 2006.

Long, Thomas. *Preaching from Memory to Hope*. Louisville: Westminster John Knox, 2009.

Lundblad, Barbara. *Transforming the Stone: Preaching through Resistance to Change*. Nashville: Abingdon, 2001.

McClure, John S. *The Round-Table Pulpit: Where Leadership and Preaching Meet*, Nashville: Abingdon, 1995.

McKenzie, Alyce M. "The Company of Sages: Homiletical Theology as a Sapiential Hermeneutic." In *Homiletical Theology: Preaching as Doing Theology*, edited by David Schnasa Jacobsen, 87–102. Eugene, OR: Cascade, 2015.

———. "'Different Strokes for Different Folks': America's Quintessential Postmodern Proverb." *Theology Today* 53 (1996) 201–12.

———. *Hear and Be Wise: Becoming a Preacher and Teacher of Wisdom*. Nashville: Abingdon, 2004.

———. *Making a Scene in the Pulpit: Vivid Preaching for Visual Learners*. Louisville: Westminster John Knox, 2018.

———. *Novel Preaching: Tips from Top Writers on Crafting Creative Sermons*. Louisville: Westminster John Knox, 2010.

———. *Preaching Biblical Wisdom in a Self-Help Society*. Nashville: Abingdon, 2002.

———. *Preaching Proverbs: Wisdom for the Pulpit*. Louisville: Westminster John Knox, 1996.

Moberly, R. W. L. "Solomon and Job: Divine Wisdom in Human Life." In *Where Shall Wisdom Be Found?: Wisdom in the Bible, the Church and the Contemporary World*, edited by Stephen C. Barton, 3–17. Edinburgh: T. & T. Clark, 1999.

Moltmann, Jürgen. *Theology of Hope*. New York: Harper & Row, 1967.

Murphy, Roland B. "Wisdom Theses." In *Wisdom and Knowledge: Papin Festschrift*, edited by Joseph Armenti, 187–200. Philadelphia: Villanova, 1976.

Myers, Ched. *Binding the Strong Man: A Political Reading of Mark's Story of Jesus*. Maryknoll, NY: Orbis, 1988.

Myers, Jacob D. *Preaching Must Die!: Troubling Homiletical Theology*. Minneapolis: Fortress, 2017.

Pape, Lance. "Commentary on Matthew 22:15–22." *Working Preacher*, October 19, 2014. https://www.workingpreacher.org/commentaries/revised-common-lectionary/ordinary-29/commentary-on-matthew-2215-22-5.

Parsons, Susan F. "Wisdom and Natural Law: A Christian Feminist Enquiry." In *Where Shall Wisdom Be Found?: Wisdom in the Bible, the Church and the Contemporary World*, edited by Stephen C. Barton, 279–94. Edinburgh: T. & T. Clark, 1999.

Peirce, C. S. *Collected Papers of Charles Sanders Peirce*. 8 vols. Edited by Charles Hartshorne et al. Cambridge, MA: Harvard University Press, 1931–1958.

Perdue, Leo G. *Wisdom and Creation: The Theology of Wisdom Literature*. Nashville: Abingdon, 1994.

Pierre, Joe. "Fake News, Echo Chambers & Filter Bubbles: A Survival Guide." *Psychology Today*, February 21, 2016. https://rsrc2.psychologytoday.com/intl/blog/psych-unseen/201611/fake-news-echo-chambers-filter-bubbles-survival-guide.

Proctor, Samuel. *Preaching about Crises in the Community*. Louisville: Westminster John Knox, 1988.

Raimi, Sam, dir. *Spider-Man*. Culver City, CA: Sony Pictures, 2002.

Resner, André. "Reading the Bible for Preaching the Gospel." Unpublished paper presented at the 2008 Annual Meeting of the Academy of Homiletics.

———. *Living In-Between: Lament, Justice, and the Persistence of the Gospel*. Eugene, OR: Wipf & Stock, 2015.

Romero, Oscar. "Lent Is the Triumph of God's Saving Plan in History." February 24, 1980. http://www.romerotrust.org.uk/sites/default/files/homilies/ART_Homilies_Vol6_187_LentIsTriumphGodsSavingPlanInHistory.pdf.

Roper, Leon Albert, and Alphonso Groenewald. "Job and Ecclesiastes as (Postmodern?) Wisdom in Revolt." *Hevormde Teologiese Studies* 69 (2013) 1–8.

Rose, Lucy Atkinson. *Sharing the Word*. Louisville: Westminster John Knox, 1997.

Schüssler Fiorenza, Elisabeth. *Jesus: Miriam's Child, Sophia's Prophet: Critical Issues in Feminist Christology*. New York: Continuum, 1994.

Simmons, Martha, and Frank Thomas, eds. *9.11.01 African American Leaders Respond to an American Tragedy*. Valley Forge, PA: Judson, 2001.

Solberg, Mary. *Compelling Knowledge: A Feminist Proposal for an Epistemology of the Cross*. Albany: State University of New York Press, 1997.

Tanaka, Sanette. "The Inner Rooms of Maya Angelou." *Wall Street Journal*, October 4, 2012. https://www.wsj.com/articles/SB10000872396390443768804578034671104895996.

Thompson, Deanna. *Crossing the Divide: Luther, Feminism, and the Cross*. Minneapolis: Fortress, 2004.

Thurman, Howard. *Jesus and the Disinherited*. New York: Abingdon-Cokesbury, 1949. Reprint, Boston: Beacon, 1996.

———. *With Head and Heart: The Autobiography of Howard Thurman*. Boston: Mariner, 1981.

Tinker, George. "Decolonizing the Language of Lutheran Theology: Confessions, Mission, Indians, and the Globalization of Hybridity." *Dialogue* 50 (2011) 193–205.

Trelstad, Marit, ed. *Cross Examinations: Readings of the Meaning of the Cross Today*. Minneapolis: Augsburg Fortress, 2006.

Volf, Miroslav. *A Public Faith: How Followers of Christ Should Serve the Common Good*. Ada, MI: Brazos, 2013.

von Rad, Gerhard. *Wisdom in Israel*. Nashville: Abingdon, 1988.

Vosoughi, Soroush, et al. "The Spread of True and False News Online." *Science* 359.6380 (March 9, 2018) 1146–51. https://science.sciencemag.org/content/359/6380/1146.

White, Adam G. *Where Is the Wise Man?: Graeco-Roman Education as a Background to the Division in 1 Corinthians 1–4*. London: Bloomsbury T. & T. Clark, 2015.

Williamson, Marianne. *A Return to Love: Reflections on the Principles of "A Course in Miracles."* New York: HarperOne, 1996.